Second Edition

TRANSFORMING
SCHOOL
CULTURE

*How to Overcome
Staff Division*

Anthony MUHAMMAD
foreword by *Richard DuFour &
Rebecca DuFour*

Solution Tree | Press

a division of

Solution Tree

555 North Morton Street
Bloomington, IN 47404
800.733.6786 (toll free) / 812.336.7700
FAX: 812.336.7790

email: info@SolutionTree.com
SolutionTree.com

Printed in the United States of America

Library of Congress Cataloging-in-Publication Data

Names: Muhammad, Anthony, author.
Title: Transforming school culture : how to overcome staff division / Anthony Muhammad.
Description: Second edition. | Bloomington, IN : Solution Tree Press, [2018] | Includes bibliographical references and index.
Identifiers: LCCN 2017013951 | ISBN 9781945349300 (perfect bound)
Subjects: LCSH: Educational leadership. | School environment. | Educational change. | Educational accountability. | School improvement programs.
Classification: LCC LB2805 .M75 2018 | DDC 371.2--dc23 LC record available at https://lccn.loc.gov/2017013951

This book is dedicated to every child who has been doubted. To all of the children in housing projects, barrios, cities, and countrysides who feel that life is hopeless, it is not hopeless! If a young man from the north end of Flint, Michigan, can be an educated scholar, the sky is the limit for you. Keep your head held high, and show the world your talent. As long as I have a breath in my body, I will fight for you, but you have to fight for yourself too.

—Anthony Muhammad

Acknowledgments

The acknowledgments for this book could easily be as long as the text. I have been so abundantly blessed, and there are so many people who have helped me grow in my short time here on this earth. First and foremost, I must give praise and all of the credit for anything worthwhile to Almighty God, the creator of all things. He has guided every step I have ever taken and every thought that I have ever produced, and to Him all praise is due.

It is with a heavy heart that I dedicate this book to my mentor and friend, Dr. Richard DuFour, who passed away on February 8, 2017. No one has ever had more influence on me professionally, and very few have influenced me more personally. I was blessed to spend fifteen years witnessing your brilliance and your example. I promise to make you proud and to be a living witness of your influence.

I must acknowledge and thank the love and influence of my grandmother, Emma Roberson-Alexander (Madear), who passed away in 2013. Special thanks to Anna Nelson, my mother, nurturer, and friend. A special, special thanks goes to my beautiful wife, Dronda. I appreciate you showing me the other side of life and for all of your patience, love, and support. Carmen, thanks for giving me the four greatest gifts that a man could ever receive. Rashad, Larry, Jamilah, Shaheed, Ayanna, and Logan, the sun rises and sets on you. There is nothing that I would not do for you. Do not be afraid to take on the world and become what God created you to be. Angie, Lee, Donald, Brandon, and Derek (RIP), thanks for supporting your big brother. Cookie, Wendy, Billie, Peter, Birdie, Ricky, and Lori, thanks for supporting your nephew.

Thanks to the entire Harper, Crawford, and Nelson families for your support and love. Thanks to the Gilliam/Hale family for accepting me into your family and giving me love and support. Finally, I would like to give special acknowledgement to my hometown of Flint, Michigan, the greatest place in the world for a young man to grow up. It breaks my heart to see the people and the city that I love suffering because of a lead-poisoned water crisis that they did not create. Every human being deserves to drink and consume clean water, and my hometown is being denied that right. I ask everyone who reads this book to join in the fight for justice for Flint! Wherever life takes me, I will be a Flintstone for life!

From a professional standpoint, I would like to thank the following powerful influences. Again, thank you, Mom, for being a great teacher and a great educational role model. I would like to express special appreciation to Becky DuFour and Robert Eaker; thank you for your guidance and willingness to share your wisdom with me. I would like to thank Luis Cruz, Mike Mattos, Ken Williams, and Sharroky Hollie for being my powerful contemporaries. I would like to express appreciation to Jeff Jones, Donald "Stubby" McLean (former director of Solution Tree Canada), and the entire Solution Tree staff.

Solution Tree Press would like to thank the following reviewers:

Nicole Airgood
Principal
Eastwood Elementary School
Sturgis, Michigan

Louis Lim
Vice Principal
Bayview Secondary School
Richmond Hill, Ontario, Canada

Doug Crowley
Assistant Principal
DeForest Area High School
DeForest, Wisconsin

Ryan Rismiller
Assistant Principal
Harding High School
Marion, Ohio

Abbey Duggins
Assistant Principal
Saluda High School
Saluda, South Carolina

Table of Contents

About the Author

Anthony Muhammad, PhD, is a much sought-after educational consultant. A practitioner for nearly twenty years, he has served as a middle school teacher, assistant principal, and principal and as a high school principal. His Transforming School Culture framework explores the root causes of staff resistance to change.

Anthony's tenure as a practitioner has earned him several awards as both a teacher and a principal. His most notable accomplishment came as principal of Levey Middle School in Southfield, Michigan, a National School of Excellence, where student proficiency on state assessments more than doubled in five years. Anthony and the staff at Levey used the Professional Learning Communities at Work® process for school improvement, and they have been recognized in several videos and articles as a model high-performing PLC.

As a researcher, Anthony has published articles in several publications in both the United States and Canada. He is author of *Transforming School Culture: How to Overcome Staff Division*; *The Will to Lead, the Skill to Teach: Transforming Schools at Every Level*; and *Overcoming the Achievement Gap Trap: Liberating Mindsets to Effect Change* and a contributor to *The Collaborative Administrator*.

To learn more about Anthony's work, visit New Frontier 21 (www
.newfrontier21.com), or follow @newfrontier21 on Twitter.

To book Anthony Muhammad for professional development, contact
pd@SolutionTree.com.

Foreword

By Richard DuFour and Rebecca DuFour

Dr. Anthony Muhammad has become a prominent voice for educational researchers and practitioners who have concluded that schools will not meet the unprecedented challenge of helping *all* students learn at high levels unless educators establish very different school cultures from those of the past. Structural changes—changes in policy, programs, schedules, and procedures—will only take a school so far. Substantive and sustainable school improvement will require educators to consider, address, and ultimately transform school culture—the assumptions, beliefs, expectations, and habits that constitute the norm for their schools.

In the second edition of *Transforming School Culture: How to Overcome Staff Division*, Dr. Muhammad provides readers with access to an updated research base and reflections on the impact of No Child Left Behind (NCLB), Race to the Top (RTTT), and the Common Core State Standards (CCSS). He challenges readers to seize the new opportunities for improving school culture as states and districts respond to the Every Student Succeeds Act (ESSA). Dr. Muhammad continues to draw on and expand on his study of thirty-four schools from around the United States—eleven elementary, fourteen middle, and nine high schools—to describe the competition and underlying tension among four different groups of educators in a school:

1. The Fundamentalists preserve the status quo. They were successful as students in the traditional school culture, and they resent any attempts to change it.

2. The Believers are committed to the learning of each student and operate under the assumption that their efforts can make an enormous difference in that learning.

3. The Tweeners are staff members who are typically new to a school and are attempting to learn its prevailing culture.

4. The Survivors are those who have been so overwhelmed by the stress and demands of the profession that their primary goal becomes making it through the day, the week, and the year.

No one who has ever worked in a school will be able to read Dr. Muhammad's descriptions without conjuring up images of specific colleagues who fall into each category. He points out, rightly, that in an organization as complex as a school, there is rarely a single "norm" that staff members embrace universally. There are, instead, *competing* assumptions, beliefs, expectations, and diverse opinions regarding such basic questions as, What is the fundamental purpose of this school? What are my responsibilities as an educator? What is the school we should strive to create? In this book, Dr. Muhammad provides strategies and guidance for transformational leaders to employ as they address the behaviors and professional learning needs of the members of each group while shaping a healthy school culture.

There is much to admire in this book. For example, Dr. Muhammad does not denigrate the members of any group. He describes educators as intelligent and concerned and acknowledges that each group is acting in accordance with what it perceives as its best interest. He emphasizes that a sense of moral purpose and the desire to help all students learn do not ensure an individual teacher is effective. He recognizes that an individual's commitment to preserving the status quo does not make that person an ineffective classroom teacher. He found very effective classroom teachers among the Fundamentalists and very ineffective teachers among the Believers, despite their good intentions. He does not depict the tension between the factions in a school as a battle of good versus evil, but rather as a struggle between real people who are merely acting in accordance with their view of the world. He is, however, emphatic in his conclusion that without changing the prevailing assumptions in most schools and ultimately changing "the way we do things around here" (page 19) educators cannot fulfill their stated purpose of helping all students learn. Thus, he sets out to help readers understand those different worldviews and offers suggestions regarding how those views might be reshaped and changed over time.

The willingness to do more than stress the importance of culture, but to present practical ideas and recommendations for influencing the existing assumptions, beliefs, expectations, and habits in a school is another of the book's strengths. Dr. Muhammad uses the research of organizational theorists to examine the different reasons people resist change. He then offers specific strategies for addressing each reason. He acknowledges there is no magic bullet that causes instant transformation, but instead advises school principals and teacher leaders—transformational leaders—regarding how they can slowly, incrementally influence assumptions and expectations until they create new norms for their schools.

Finally, the book is particularly powerful because the author has not merely studied the challenge of changing a school's culture; he has actually done it in an extraordinarily successful way. Dr. Muhammad, a former Principal of the Year for the state of Michigan, led a staff in transforming a high-poverty, high-minority school with a toxic culture of low expectations and a tradition of miserable student achievement into a nationally recognized school that serves as a model for successfully closing the achievement gap. When Dr. Muhammad states that a "dysfunctional or toxic school culture is not insurmountable" (page 22), he does so with the absolute conviction of someone who has been spectacularly successful in taking on that challenge.

Be forewarned that this book is provocative. Dr. Muhammad offers bold statements, and it is very likely that you will not concur with all of his observations and conclusions. You will, however, be required to think and to examine your own beliefs.

For too long, educators have given lip service to the idea of creating schools where all students learn at high levels. For too long, we have devoted time to developing pious mission statements rather than aligning our practices with that mission. For too long, we have tinkered with the structures of our schools and focused on projects or goals that have no impact on student learning. For too long, we have ignored the elephant in the room and avoided the crucial conversations regarding the assumptions, expectations, and beliefs that underlie our practices. Dr. Muhammad issues a passionate call for all educators to confront the fierce urgency of now and to take meaningful steps that breathe new life into schools and the students they serve. We urge you to read this book and heed his words.

Introduction

A lot has changed since 2009, including the importance of school culture. The challenges facing educators have become even more daunting, and the need for staff cohesion has become even more imperative. This edition will explore the impact of internal and external factors that have provided challenges and opportunities in the development of school culture.

Public policy has a tremendous effect on school function. No Child Left Behind (NCLB) challenged the status quo of education in positive and negative ways. NCLB was replaced with the Every Student Succeeds Act (ESSA) in 2017, which will again have an impact on school funding. The Great Recession of 2007–2009 also impacted public policy and funding, and shaped the goals, focus, and culture of schools.

In 2009, *Transforming School Culture* provided educators with a context to understand the behaviors and motivations of their colleagues, and a road map to how to overcome clashes and division. Since 2009, more studies have validated the importance of school culture in student performance; most notably the work of John Hattie and his *Visible Learning* research in 2012. In this edition, I provide more insight into ways to transform culture in the light of the new challenges and research. The integrity of the first edition remains intact, and the second edition builds on that foundation to provide a modern context.

This second edition has the following additions and revisions.

- New insights into the four types of educators (Believers, Fundamentalists, Tweeners, and Survivors)

- An updated research base, including over thirty new references

- Connections to ESSA and CCSS

- Reflections on NCLB's impact on education

- Further guidance on what it takes to be a transformational leader and how to redirect Fundamentalists through communication, trust, capacity, and accountability

- A new chapter of frequently asked questions in regard to school culture, leadership, and the four types of educators

Chapter 1 first presents the consistent cultural reform that must take place in the U.S. public school system for schools to arm all students with the 21st century skills they need to succeed in the ever-changing world they face. After that, chapter 2 displays the framework of a modern school culture and identifies the factors—both internal and external—that make school cultural transformation difficult; when educators examine their current behaviors and their school's conditions, they can better strategize to form a healthy public school environment. Chapters 3–6 identify the characteristics that make each group's behaviors, actions, and attitudes distinct and that impact a school culture. Chapter 3 addresses the Believers, seasoned educators who make key school decisions and therefore play the largest role in achieving higher levels of student performance and satisfaction. Chapter 4 discusses Tweeners; schools must fortify the bonds built between a school and a Tweener to help growth and reform take place. Chapter 5 next considers the Survivors; their lack of good professional practice hugely impacts the quality of students' education. Then, chapter 6 covers the type of educator that poses the biggest threat to school culture improvements: the Fundamentalist. Chapter 7 shows readers how to help Fundamentalist educators drop their long-held, unintentionally toxic practices; actively reform their mindsets; and seek a more productive, unified methodology that produces greater student achievement. Chapter 8 covers practical methods that school administrators and teachers can use to foster a collective sense of purpose among leaders, teachers, and students and maintain a healthy school culture focused on student learning. Finally, chapter 9 offers answers to questions I have frequently been asked since the first edition of *Transforming School Culture* was released in 2009. These questions and answers center on school culture, leadership, Believers, Tweeners, Survivors, and Fundamentalists.

The book includes an appendix that features specific details regarding my formal and informal observations of thirty-four schools across the United States and how the behavior of the schools' staff supported or hindered student achievement.

As you delve into the following chapters, consider my hope for this book: that educators dedicate themselves to creating schools that provide guidance and support for all students. These schools, that ensure learning for all, are transformational institutions that make the community and our world a better place to live in.

CHAPTER 1

From Status Quo to True Reform

For more than a century, educators, scholars, politicians, and citizens have debated the purpose of our public school system and how best to reform it. Ironically, our public school system has undergone sweeping changes, yet it has remained largely the same, and there is still a lack of clear consensus about what is needed to ensure that all our schools perform at high levels and all our students achieve success.

Education has traditionally been viewed as the best route for social mobility, but for some young people, this route is not accessible. In fact, an abundance of data on the costs of this failure of our education system shows the system is absolutely broken. This is especially true for students from certain demographic groups who have been traditionally underserved by our school system.

Persistent gaps between white and black citizens in critical areas like income, health, and education have been important issues at the center of debates about equity for a long time. A report from the Pew Research Center (2016) finds that these gaps are as large as ever. Specifically:

- African American citizens are twice as likely to be poor compared to white citizens.

- African American median income is half of white median income.

- White median net worth is thirteen times the net worth of the average African American household.

- The nonmarital African American birthrate is twice the white rate.

- African American children are three times more likely to live in a single-parent home than white children.

- The home ownership gap between African American and white citizens is nearly 30 percent.

These statistics are even more shocking considering the fact that these gaps actually increased over the eight years under the presidency of Barack Obama, the nation's first African American president (Pew Research Center, 2016). President Obama spent a significant portion of his professional career as a community organizer on the south side of Chicago, where he witnessed the poverty and struggles of African American communities with underperforming schools. In fact, he describes the interaction with that community as the epiphany that led him to politics and public service (Obama, 2008). It would only seem logical, based on President Obama's own words, that this community would expect more policy advocacy under his administration.

The Latino population in America has grown rapidly, and Latinos now represent the largest ethnic minority group in the United States. America's Latino population is now facing the issues that have plagued African Americans. The same Pew Research Center (2016) report reveals:

- Latino high school graduation rates have doubled since the 1970s, yet they still graduate at two-thirds the rate of white students.

- White students are twice as likely to graduate from college than Latino students.

- Latino median income is 61 percent of white median income.

- Latino citizens are twice as likely to live in poverty than white citizens.

- The home ownership gap between Latino and white citizens is nearly 30 percent.

However, race is just one risk factor. Students from poor families, regardless of their racial group, are experiencing significant difficulties. The U.S. Census Bureau reports that economically disadvantaged white households (those with incomes below the national poverty line) have significant gaps in income, employment, and health compared to national averages, though not as pronounced as African Americans and Latinos (Proctor, Semega, & Kollar, 2016). And there is evidence that poverty can put children more at risk for outcomes even more serious than low income and unemployment. A 2005 study with more than thirty-four thousand patients with mental illness proves that children who grow up in impoverished homes are significantly more likely to develop mental illness than children who grow up in homes with incomes above the national poverty line. Christopher G. Hudson (2005) writes, "The poorer one's socioeconomic conditions are, the higher one's risk is for mental disability and psychiatric hospitalization" (p. 14).

Professor of economics and education Henry Levin (2006) identifies links between high school graduation and quality of life. While analyzing the effects of failing to complete high school, he finds that minority students and students of poverty have much lower graduation rates than the U.S. average. In fact, African American and Latino students graduate from high school at a rate slightly above 50 percent (compared to the national graduation rate of 70 percent), while economically disadvantaged students graduate at a rate of 63 percent. He finds that adults without a high school diploma are twice as likely to be unemployed as high school graduates. The life expectancy of a high school dropout as compared to a graduate is 9.2 years lower, and the average sixty-five-year-old high school graduate is in better health than the average forty-five-year-old high school dropout. Finally, a 2014 Brookings Institution report finds that 70 percent of those sitting in U.S. prisons are high school dropouts (Kearney & Harris, 2014). In the words of the crew aboard the *Apollo 13* spacecraft, "Houston, we have a problem!" The youth who need education most to provide a catalyst for creating positive change in their lives are those who persistently achieve at the lowest levels in our schools.

Trends have shown that student academic outcomes have not improved for society's most vulnerable students. The U.S. Department of Education's Office for Civil Rights (OCR) released a report in March of 2014 that delivers somber news. The report, *Civil Rights Data Collection for the 2013–14 School Year*, includes findings from every U.S. public school, totaling about forty-nine million students (OCR, 2014a). Following are some of the key findings.

- Among high schools serving the highest percentage of African American and Latino students, one in three do not offer a single chemistry course, and one in four do not offer a course more advanced than algebra 1.

- In schools that offer "gifted and talented" programs, African American and Latino students represent 40 percent of students but only 26 percent of those enrolled in such programs.

- African American, Latino, and impoverished students attend schools with higher concentrations of first-year teachers than do white students.

- Students with disabilities are more than twice as likely to be suspended from school as those without disabilities.

- African American students are suspended and expelled from school at a rate more than three times as high as white students (16 percent versus 5 percent).

Student performance in mathematics and reading has always been an acceptable measure of student progress in school. One measure, which has been widely accepted as objective, is the U.S. Department of Education's National Assessment of Educational Progress (NAEP), which it administers to students in grades 4, 8, and 12 from a random selection of students in all fifty states. It is also known as the Nation's Report Card because it provides scholars, practitioners, and lawmakers with a broad picture of educational trends in the United States. The assessment shows that the academic achievement of African American, Latino, and impoverished students has steadily improved over a twenty-year period of time (Lee, 2014). But, the assessment also shows that the gains are not outpacing the growth of other student groups, so the gaps are still very large. The 2011 NAEP results reveal that the average score of African American and Latino students in fourth- and eighth-grade mathematics and reading compared to white students is over twenty points lower, equivalent to performing over two grade levels behind. The twelfth-grade scores reveal a gap of over forty points in mathematics and reading, equivalent to over four grade levels behind, resulting in what is popularly called *the four-year gap*—meaning that the average African American and Latino high school senior has mathematics and reading skills equivalent to the skills of an average white eighth grader (National Center for Education Statistics [NCES], 2015).

Challenges of the 21st Century

As journalist and three-time Pulitzer Prize winner Thomas L. Friedman (2005) acknowledges in his book *The World Is Flat: A Brief History of the Twenty-First Century*, the 21st century landscape has changed. Foreign competition, especially in the areas of technology and science, has increased substantially. As corporations struggle to find educated and skilled workers, they are looking to the shores of foreign nations more and more. Friedman (2005) points to the increase in technology worldwide as a catalyst for a world without borders. The Internet, satellites, and global technology have made it possible for workers to utilize their talents from a foreign shore without ever setting foot in the United States.

What does this mean for the American economy? Corporations, by nature, seek to be profitable. They want to maximize productivity and minimize expenses. The days of industrial plants filled with high-paying, low-skill jobs are over. The safety net for those who occupy the lowest space on the educational and societal bell curve is gone. Companies are seeking employees who have academic skills, common sense, and social skills, and if they have to recruit overseas to accomplish this, they are willing to do so. Nations like India and China are providing workers who have the kind of skills that companies want, and they are increasing their recruitment efforts globally in order to fill this need (Majumdar, 2013).

This is especially bad news for the United States' poor and disenfranchised. With more skilled workers making their entrance into the global workforce, education is more critical than ever. As the data show, opportunities are already limited for poor and minority citizens in the United States, and globalization signifies more of the same. By the year 2020, 65 percent of American jobs will require some form of postsecondary education (Carnevale, Smith, & Strohl, 2010).

We should never consider education a luxury; it is a necessity, especially for children in poor and minority communities. It may be their only chance at a better life. So why are the schools that serve these students, on average, in the worst condition, and why do they have the lowest levels of funding and academic achievement? School funding for the typical urban public school is on average 30 percent less than suburban schools that serve primarily white middle-class students. In fact, a group of students from the Chicago Public Schools boycotted the first day of school in protest of the huge funding disparity between the per-pupil funding in Chicago ($10,400) and the nearby suburban district of New Trier Township ($17,000) (Sadovi, 2008).

So what does all this mean for American schools? It means that they have to respond like never before. Michael Fullan (2003) writes in *The Moral Imperative of School Leadership*, "The best case for public education has always been that it is a common good. Everyone, ultimately has a stake in the caliber of schools, and education is everyone's business" (p. 14). The United States built its reputation and status worldwide on the backs of its citizens' ingenuity and work ethic. With other nations now seeking to distinguish themselves among the world's elite, how will our schools respond? Do we simply believe that we are entitled to world admiration, or will our schools and our society rise to the occasion and produce better results—more skilled and focused students?

If the United States is to maintain its position in the world, the quality of education and academic skills of its students must improve. In addition, more students—not just white, middle-class, and affluent students—have to develop educationally so that America can continue to compete and be a viable force in our new global economy. Racism and class bias cannot be obstacles that interfere with education but unfortunately, they are. "Education for all" is not just a liberal rant; it is a matter of survival for everyone, but especially those groups that have been pushed into the margins of society.

There are examples of societies that have accepted the challenge to improve the educational experiences of their students and achieved great success. Finland, a northern European nation, moved from relative educational obscurity in the 1980s, to an educational powerhouse. Pasi Sahlberg (2011), an official with the Finnish Ministry of

Education, documents the rise of the Finnish educational system in his book *Finnish Lessons: What Can the World Learn From Educational Change in Finland?* Sahlberg (2011) refers to the *Finnish way* as a collection of five principles that guided the three-decade ascension of the Finnish school system.

1. Customizing teaching and learning

2. Focusing on creative learning

3. Encouraging risk taking

4. Learning from the past and owning innovations

5. Sharing responsibility and trust

The Finnish way is a cooperative endeavor that takes into consideration that the school system is a very important part of a network of systems, including economic, political, social, and health. The government had a vested interest in working with schools in a collaborative partnership to improve their performance, which in turn, would improve society. Their destinies were linked, and they created policies and conditions that improved their schools' performance.

Sahlberg (2011) is critical of the approach of the United States, England, Canada, and many other industrialized nations, which he calls the *Global Educational Reform Movement* (GERM). The five principles of GERM are in direct contradiction to the Finnish way.

1. Standardized teaching and learning

2. Focus on literacy and numeracy

3. Prescribed curriculum

4. Market-oriented reform ideas

5. Test-based accountability and control

Sahlberg (2011) points out that GERM is based on external drivers, like fear of punishment or the benefit of public praise associated with performance on standardized academic tests. These drivers isolate schools as independent units, left on their own to improve and solely motivated by rewards or punishments that their government administers. NCLB sought to ensure student proficiency in mathematics and reading in every American public school by 2014, but the drivers of fear and reward are not good drivers, especially in motivating educators to embrace the changes in practice necessary to ensure this noble goal. This approach disconnects the government from its schools, rather than using an integrated approach with mutual respect and accountability like Finland practices. As Michael Fullan (2011) writes:

> There is no way that these ambitions and admirable nationwide goals will be met with the strategies being used. No successful system has ever been led with these drivers. They cannot generate on a large scale the kind of intrinsic motivational energy that will be required to transform these massive systems. The US and Australian aspirations sound great as goals, but crumble from a strategy or driver perspective. (p. 7)

The major difference between the Finnish way and GERM is an investment in cultivating an environment of change through investments in people. Michael Fullan warns in his statement that no successful system has ever been led by these drivers (fear and reward). Although, the United States chose GERM principles, and the results have been very dismal based on the ever-increasing achievement gap data cited earlier in this chapter.

From No Child Left Behind to Every Student Succeeds

The reauthorization in 2001 of the Elementary and Secondary Education Act (ESEA), also known as No Child Left Behind (NCLB), symbolized a huge shift in the focus of American schools. This law, which required all students in America's public schools to perform at a proficient level on each state's standardized assessment in reading and mathematics by 2014 or face sanctions, sent a shockwave through the U.S. public school system. NCLB guided U.S. education policy until 2015, when it was replaced with the Every Student Succeeds Act (ESSA), which President Barack Obama signed on December 10, 2015. Many view ESSA as the state version of NCLB and not much different than its predecessor (Greene, 2017).

Implementing NCLB meant that for the first time in U.S. history, schools would be judged based on *student outcomes*, not *educator intentions.* Many wondered if a government mandate was enough to change long-standing gaps in student achievement and change the nature of teaching and learning in the classroom. That was a very good question. In fact, during NCLB's implementation, students, parents, and educators saw no significant progress in closing achievement gaps in student performance, and have made no real progress in realizing the fair and equitable system the legislation claimed to champion.

As a historical look at the impact of NCLB, and its transition to ESSA, consider the 2007 NAEP. According to the data, students from inner-city schools were making modest gains in the areas of mathematics and reading, especially in the early grades, compared to NAEP achievement levels over the previous seven years, but absolutely no progress in secondary grades in the same period. These incremental gains in the early grades were admirable, but they were not growing at the same rate as gains made in economically affluent suburban schools with majority white and Asian populations, so even small signs of progress did little to close performance gaps between inner-city and suburban students (Zuckerbrod, 2007). And the fear of accountability and public embarrassment over decreasing student test scores under NCLB created a high level of *data anxiety* among school officials (Earl & Katz, 2006). Under NCLB, districts became increasingly savvy at hiding their struggling students or finding ways to omit them from their test results altogether. A 2006 study finds that over two million student scores, almost exclusively minority and socioeconomically disadvantaged students, were "mysteriously omitted" from state test reporting data to the federal government (Dizon, Feller, & Bass, 2006).

To add insult to injury, an *Associated Press* poll finds that the majority of teachers (58 percent) felt that being expected to ensure that all of their students read and perform mathematics at grade level was unrealistic and impossible to accomplish (Feller, 2006). Organizational protection for marginally performing teachers also made implementing NCLB's goals difficult. The New York Teacher Project Fund's study of five large school systems finds that union staffing rules often allow veteran teachers to transfer to new assignments without giving administrators a say in the matter (Helfand, 2005). Because it is difficult to fire poorly performing teachers, principals often move such employees from school to school. As a result, many urban schools were forced to staff their schools with teachers who are not wanted elsewhere. Michelle Rhee, the founder of the study's sponsoring organization, states that "without changing these labor rules, urban schools will never be in a position to sustain meaningful school reform" (Helfand, 2005, p. 1). These facts should make us question our seriousness as a profession and as a nation about creating schools that guarantee learning for all students.

NCLB's goals were admirable and morally correct, but we must acknowledge that breaking a system of normally distributed achievement was not going to end with the stroke of a legislative pen. In *Tinkering Toward Utopia*, a watershed book on the history of educational reform in the United States, David Tyack and Larry Cuban (1995) clearly establish that educational reform is very difficult to establish, and very little has changed in the American education system since its original construction in the late 19th century. Tyack and Cuban (1995) point to the complex nature of our society along with the ever-changing definition of the public schools' purpose as causing a stalemate that is very difficult to overcome. These issues are woven into the fabric of American public education. A solid, realistic plan of action that aggressively addresses these issues is necessary for true reform.

By all accounts, NCLB was a miserable failure, as FairTest: The National Center for Fair and Open Testing notes in its 2012 analysis, *NCLB's Lost Decade for Educational Progress: What Can We Learn From This Policy Failure?* (Guisbond, 2012). Its analysis reveals that NCLB has not improved student performance in mathematics and reading, and the law led to some unintended consequences that created even more problems.

- An overemphasis on standardized test scores as the primary measure of student achievement led to underfunding arts education in school, teaching to the test, states lowering academic rigor to improve passage rates, and schools manipulating student test scores (cheating).

- An overemphasis on school accountability ratings associated with standardized test scores led to massive student *push-outs.* Students who were unlikely to pass state standardized tests saw an increase in disciplinary suspension and expulsion, placement in alternative education programs, and interactions with the criminal justice system (school-to-prison pipeline).

- An overemphasis on mathematics and reading led to neglecting the students' holistic needs. Programs aimed at addressing students' social and emotional needs were underfunded to fund more supplementary services for mathematics and reading improvement. Mathematics and reading are very important measures of student success, but redistributing funds earmarked for social and emotional needs created the unintended consequence of eliminating or underfunding important student support systems like after-school programs.

ESSA is not very different, in substance, than NCLB. ESSA still requires states to test students annually in mathematics and reading and to target schools that are low performing and mandate a plan of improvement (The Alliance, 2016). The only real substantive difference is that the oversight of school progress, primarily based on standardized test scores, shifts from the federal government to the states (Klein, 2016). States' rights advocates and those who are skeptical about federal intervention in educational policy applaud ESSA as a significant improvement over NCLB (Martin & Sargrad, 2015). But, not everyone is convinced that simply changing the system of oversight from the federal to the state level is a good idea and will benefit the neediest students. Leslie Proll, former director of policy for the NAACP Legal Defense and Educational Fund, notes:

> The whole purpose behind the original bill (NCLB) was to ensure that there were consistent standards and federal oversight to make sure that states and localities were doing the right thing by poor children, by children who needed that assistance the most, and reducing that and granting so much discretion to states is just worrisome. (as cited in Davis, 2015)

I agree with Proll's assessment; ESSA will not be any more beneficial to our most vulnerable populations than NCLB. Bringing educational equity to fruition will require more than changing school oversight from the federal to the state level.

In 2008, Janet Napolitano, governor of Arizona at the time and the chairperson of the National Governors Association, initiated a task force of U.S. secretaries of education to investigate creating national educational standards (Conley, 2014). The U.S. Constitution does not specifically grant the federal government jurisdiction over educational policy, so the omission makes education policy a right of the states. Governor Napolitano was concerned that under NCLB, schools would be rated and federal funding would be tied to standardized test scores. Her greatest concern was the fact that all fifty states had different curriculum standards and fifty different standardized tests. On June 2, 2010, the task force introduced a set of academic standards in mathematics and English language arts that would be later known as the Common Core State Standards, which forty-two states and the District of Columbia would adopt. These states also agreed to assess the standards on one of two standardized tests—from (1) the Smarter Balanced Assessment Consortium (SBAC) or (2) the Partnership for Assessment of Readiness for College and Careers (PARCC)—in small state clusters, in order to learn from one another and share good practice and policy across states (Conley, 2014). States that agreed to participate were promised a share of $350 million earmarked under a federal incentive program called Race to the Top (RTTT).

The intention of the National Governors Association was to ensure curricular equity across state lines and analyze student performance data that were rooted in the same content and rigor. Rick Hess, the director of educational policy at the American Enterprise Institute, recognized that Napolitano's fight would be much more political than educational: "The problem with that is if you had hard tests or hard standards you made your schools look bad. So there was a real, kind of perverse incentive baked into NCLB" (as cited in Bidwell, 2014). Dane Linn, the vice president of the Business Roundtable, echoed some of the same concerns that Hess shared:

> What's more important? To tell the truth to parents about where their kids are really performing? Or to continue to make them believe they're doing really well, only until they get into

the workforce or they go to college and they're finding out they need to be put in a remedial English class? (as cited in Bidwell, 2014)

By 2013, many states that adopted the CCSS in 2010 started to ditch them or modify their commitment. States like Indiana, South Carolina, and Oklahoma passed legislation that either withdrew their participation altogether or weakened their financial support and commitment. The decline of the enthusiasm for the CCSS movement can be traced to four important realities (Jochim & McGuinn, 2016).

1. Far-right politics framed the CCSS and the financial incentives as a federal attempt to take over locally controlled schools.

2. Far-left politics framed the CCSS and the assessments associated with them as an attempt to use performance data to evaluate teacher performance and undermine the power of unions.

3. The standards were developed privately, and there was no open public debate. The public did not have a personal stake in their adoption and implementation.

4. The development and implementation of the two assessments were sloppy, with many logistical and technical glitches which annoyed educational professionals, and they lost their enthusiasm over time. By 2016, thirty-eight states had left one or both of the testing consortia.

The Dawn of a New Day

I first heard of NCLB on an ordinary Friday morning in March of 2002 while serving as a middle school principal in an urban school district with more than 98 percent minority enrollment. I was on my way to the district administrative office for our biweekly administrator's meeting, called the *pay-day meeting*. It was 8:05 a.m., and I was five minutes late, as usual. I was expecting an agenda filled with mundane administrative logistics and announcements. I anticipated the superintendent leading the meeting, as he usually did, with concerns about our budget or some security issue from a sporting event. There was no way I could have anticipated the topic of this meeting.

As I entered the room, the superintendent introduced an official from the Michigan Department of Education who came to share some information from the federal government. As she explained the goals and components of a new law, NCLB, there was an eerie silence in the room coupled with a universal feeling of shock and anxiety.

This law's goals were not incongruent with what we, as administrators, wanted for each one of our students, but we never suspected that we would actually be held legally accountable for producing schools that made these wishes a reality. The state official went on to explain that schools that did not meet these requirements would be labeled as *failing* and would face a series of sanctions.

Everyone at the meeting was shocked. Our effectiveness or proficiency would be judged primarily by student outcomes on standardized tests and our ability to move our entire school organization to accept this new reality. We had been introduced to the new reality of American education. After examining our reality, it seemed we had to be miracle workers to bring this new reality to fruition.

Why was there so much shock and anxiety among this group of administrators? Primarily, we were anxious because we were painfully aware of the culture and history of our schools. We were aware of what we assumed government officials were not. We were aware of all the issues surrounding teacher quality, staff expectations, student apathy, and inadequate parental support, among other things that we had worked so hard to keep away from the public eye. We had been trained to create an illusion of prosperity that we never expected to actually achieve. We knew that there were many classrooms where the curriculum was not followed. We knew that gaps in student performance were expected in a traditional urban public school system. We were being asked to do something that no one had ever been asked to do: create a functional system in which every student could learn and would learn, despite the many obstacles and the myriad of tasks necessary just to be functional. It was absolutely overwhelming, and we did not know where to start. In fact, we banked on the assumption that if we ignored this new law long enough, it would eventually just go away.

Clearly, it has not gone away, and years later, the same anxiety exists. We are just as confused today as we were on that memorable Friday morning in 2002. ESSA, which is essentially the state version of NCLB, has done little to soothe that initial anxiety. Student performance has improved very little, and the dysfunction in our education system that faced us in 2002 is still prevalent. In fact, former U.S. Secretary of Education Margaret Spellings told a group of businesspeople in Detroit that "we can't adequately solve this problem [the achievement gap] until we diagnose what's wrong" (as cited in Higgins & Pratt-Dawsey, 2008, p. 1). Many years and several billion dollars later, our best educational minds are still diagnosing the problem. Improving public schools is very complex indeed.

As Margaret Spellings points out, understanding and diagnosing the problem will help us start the much-needed process of reconstructing our schools so that the organization meets the varied needs of all students (as cited in Higgins & Pratt-Dawsey, 2008). This book contends that this very difficult journey begins with the adults, the professionals, taking an honest look at how this gap in student performance began and how it is perpetuated despite the honest efforts of very intelligent and concerned people. Universal achievement remains a pipe dream until we take an honest look at our beliefs, practices, behaviors, and the norms of our organization. These elements make up a very sensitive system known as a school's culture. This is where many school officials and reformers fear to tread, but it is this place that holds the biggest keys to unlocking the potential of our public schools.

School Culture Research

In my work, I hear people use the terms *culture* and *climate* synonymously, and they are very different. In short, *culture* is how we *behave*, and *climate* is how we *feel*. Culture is "the way we do things around here," and climate is "the way we feel around here" (Gruenert & Whitaker, 2015, p. 10). It is very possible that a group of professionals could *feel* very good about themselves and their students but still fail to modify their behaviors and practices and see no substantive change. The flattening world, described earlier in this chapter by Thomas Friedman through the lens of globalization, and the economic and social challenges of our world demand that schools make substantive improvements so that students have a fighting chance in a world that continues to become more competitive. Simply feeling better about ourselves is not enough. It is going to take a deep reflection of our individual and collective behaviors and creating conditions that allow all of us to improve our practices and behaviors.

According to Kent D. Peterson, educational consultant and professor, "School culture is the set of norms, values and beliefs, rituals and ceremonies, symbols and stories that make up the 'persona' of the school" (as cited in Cromwell, 2002). For years, we did not consider how the varied and diverse human elements from stakeholders—students, parents, and educators—impacted our schools. But we do now.

Peterson's explanation of school culture is functional and accurately describes how the unseen human factors of a school affect the day-to-day practices and behaviors within a school (as cited in Cromwell, 2002). Peterson categorizes school culture into two types: (1) positive and (2) toxic. He describes a *positive* culture as one where:

> There's an informal network of heroes and heroines and an informal grapevine that passes along information about what's going on in the school . . . [a] set of values that supports professional development of teachers, a sense of responsibility for student learning, and a positive, caring atmosphere. (as cited in Cromwell, 2002)

In essence, he is saying that a *positive* school culture is a place where:

- Educators have an unwavering belief in the ability of all their students to achieve success, and they pass that belief on to others in overt and covert ways.

- Educators create policies and procedures and adopt practices that support their belief in every student's ability.

Richard DuFour, Robert Eaker, and Rebecca DuFour describe the cultural conditions necessary to create a powerful school in a way similar to Peterson (DuFour, 2015; DuFour & Eaker, 1998; DuFour, DuFour, & Eaker, 2008). In order for a school to be a place that provides high levels of learning for all students regardless of student background, the staff must articulate through their behavior the beliefs that:

- All students can learn.

- All students will learn because of what we do.

DuFour, DuFour, Eaker, Many, and Mattos (2016) argue that not only must staff hold as their fundamental belief that each student has the ability to learn, but members must also organize to utilize their resources to support that singular focus.

On the flip side, Peterson describes a *toxic* culture as one where "teacher relations are often conflictual, the staff doesn't believe in the ability of the students to succeed and a generally negative attitude prevails" (as cited in Cromwell, 2002). That is, in a toxic culture:

- Educators believe that student success is based on students' level of concern, attentiveness, prior knowledge, and willingness to comply with the demands of the school, and they articulate that belief in overt and covert ways.

- Educators create policies and procedures and adopt practices that support their belief in the impossibility of universal achievement.

Peterson accurately describes the characteristics and function of school culture (as cited in Cromwell, 2002). Descriptions are helpful and provide a good starting point, but descriptions alone are inadequate to initiate transformation. I contend that in order to transform school culture, we must do more than analyze its characteristics and functionality; we must also trace its development and the educator's motivation for hanging on to paradigms that are contrary to those articulated in the public belief statements of the school or district as an organization.

The Importance of Closing the Gap

Research has been helpful in exposing the significant power school culture wields in the functioning of schools. In fact, the American Sociological Association finds that a school's level of efficacy and its collectively held expectations for student success may be the leading indicator in whether students attend postsecondary education (Jones,

2008). What is not so evident, and is perhaps even controversial, is that educators' personal belief systems may be the most powerful variables perpetuating learning gaps in our public school system. Traditional legislative mandates that focus solely on student outcomes, even when coupled with threats of embarrassment and loss of job security, may be powerless to effect change in the face of personal belief systems that perpetuate the achievement gap. In fact, this book will contend that dysfunctional school cultures create systems that maintain the gap. Mary Kennedy (2005) writes, "The traditional induction to teaching encourages teachers to rely on their own prior beliefs and values for guidance and to think of their practice as a highly personal and idiosyncratic endeavor" (p. 11). School culture is indeed a delicate web of past personal experience, organizational history, and interaction with the greater society; however, I contend that dysfunctional or toxic school culture is not insurmountable. As we shall see, many aspects of human behavior, social conditions, and history suggest that these types of environments can be transformed.

This book's goal is twofold: (1) to provide a framework for understanding how school cultures operate from a political and sociological perspective and (2) to offer practical strategies to manipulate that culture in order to intentionally create positive atmospheres that not only tolerate change but that seek and embrace the changes that maximize organizational effectiveness.

Technical Change Versus Cultural Change

To clarify the power of school culture, I must first identify the two types of organizational change prevalent in today's schools: (1) technical and (2) cultural change. *Technical changes* are changes to the tools or mechanisms professionals use to do their jobs effectively. These changes within a school context refer to changes in structure, policies, or teaching tools (for example, changing from a six-period school day to a block schedule, revising the curriculum with changes in learning standards or text material, or offering more advanced and rigorous classes, to name a few). These changes are definitely necessary to effect improvement in student performance, but they produce very few positive results when people who do not believe in the intended outcome of the change use them.

In *The Advantage: Why Organizational Health Trumps Everything Else in Business*, Patrick Lencioni (2012) examines the difference between these two constructs. He seeks to understand why some companies tended to have an advantage in the marketplace and outperformed similar companies in similar markets. He observes that success requires two systemic elements: *smart* (technical) and *health* (culture). His investigation reveals that most companies chose the smart route and devalued the health of the organization, and that was a big mistake. Companies that had an advantage focused heavily on the human, or healthy, side of the organization and built human capital to provide the context for the implementation of smart innovation. He finds five key experiences in healthy companies.

1. Minimal politics

2. Minimal confusion

3. High morale

4. High productivity

5. Low employee turnover

The organization's health ultimately leads to improvements in innovation (smart), producing better results and greater longevity. Lencioni (2012) concludes that innovation and intellect do not lead to greater levels of productivity if they are implemented within a context that is unhealthy. Health has to come before intellect. Innovation has a fighting chance if it is being implemented within a healthy human environment. He warns that developing the health (culture) of an organization is difficult because human beings are difficult and complex beings:

> Most people prefer to look for answers where the light is better, where they are more comfortable. And the light is certainly better in the measurable, objective, and data-driven world of organizational intelligence (the smart side of the equation) than it is in the messier, more unpredictable world of organizational health. (Lencioni, 2012, p. 7)

Technical changes have become very popular in public schools, especially since the passage of NCLB and ESSA. Why would educators continue to seek these surface-level changes when the United States has such a long history of initiatives that eventually overwhelm our school system's culture of low efficacy? Central leadership and site leadership have scrambled to find programs or initiatives that will be the magic bullet to fix all ailments. Terms like *research-based* and *best practice* have been no match for the deeply ingrained disbelief in student ability that cripples many struggling schools. In fact, I have had the opportunity to study several schools where pessimistic faculty members are eager to prove that new strategies or programs aimed at raising student performance do not work in order to justify and solidify their hypothesis that not all students are capable of achieving excellence.

A report from the Institute of Education Sciences (IES) reveals that the highly regarded Reading First literacy initiative, a cornerstone of President George W. Bush's education policy, had little to no effect on student reading proficiency (Toppo, 2008). In fact, the study goes on to claim that students who received services under this initiative, which had an annual cost of over $1 billion, performed no better than students who had no exposure to this reading intervention. The evidence is clear: these types of so-called research-based strategies are no match for elements of culture that help maintain gaps in student achievement.

The Impact of Beliefs

Some might assume that mere belief in a concept or reality has little effect on a person or group's ability to achieve that reality. The research teaches us something very different. John Hattie has been credited with publishing the most definitive evidence of the factors that affect student learning outcomes in recorded history. Hattie (2012) researches and synthesizes eight hundred meta-analyses measuring the effect of 195 factors that impact student learning. This meta-analysis took fifteen years to complete, and Hattie released his findings in a series of books known as *Visible Learning*.

Hattie (2012) measures the impact of many important factors in predicting and influencing student learning. Some of those factors are environmental, economic, professional, and cultural. He identifies the impact of each factor by assigning an *effect size* to each factor. In the book *Visible Learning for Teachers: Maximizing Impact on Learning*, the top-three factors are all related to culture and belief of student achievement.

1. Teacher estimates of achievement—1.62

2. Collective teacher efficacy—1.57

3. Student estimate of achievement or self-reported grades—1.44

Students will learn more and be more successful in an environment where all educators *believe* they can learn at high levels and those educators work together to convince the students that they can achieve lofty academic goals teachers set for them. A leader who understands how to cultivate this type of culture will place a school clearly on the path to improvement and sustainable growth. The skills necessary to create a healthy culture are very different than the ineffective and destructive path to change that we have taken in the past.

Cultural change is a much more difficult form of change to accomplish. It cannot be gained through force or coercion (like NCLB or ESSA). As human beings, we do not have the ability to control the thoughts and beliefs of others, so cultural change requires something more profound. It requires leaders to become adept at gaining cooperation and skilled in the arts of diplomacy, salesmanship, patience, endurance, and encouragement. It takes knowledge of where a school has been, and agreement about where the school should go. It requires an ability to deal with beliefs, policies, and institutions that have been established to buffer educators from change and accountability. It is a tightrope act of major proportion. But cultural change must be achieved—and it must be achieved well—if we are to prepare our current and future generations of students for an ever-changing world that is becoming more demanding each day. Substantial cultural change must precede technical change. When a school has a healthy culture, the professionals within it will seek the tools that they need to accomplish their goal of universal student achievement; they will give a school new life by overcoming the staff division that halts transformation.

CHAPTER 2

The Framework of Modern School Culture

School culture is a complex web of history, psychology, sociology, economics, and political science. To effectively diagnose and eliminate toxic school culture, we must take an honest look at the internal and external factors that create the conditions that make cultural transformation difficult.

Schools in the Era of Accountability

The accountability movement, and No Child Left Behind and the Every Student Succeeds Act in particular, did not create the cultural issues confronting today's school system. But this new era has brought some deeply rooted belief systems and practices to the forefront for examination, including issues such as how we analyze, staff, and fund schools. Examining the current environment and conditions in our schools can help us understand the myriad paradigms that exist within the walls of our public schools and therefore help us strategize to transform the environment into a healthy one.

Who Is to Blame?

No Child Left Behind and the Every Student Succeeds Act mandate the school as the responsible party when it comes to effectiveness. This is very different from the traditional belief that students and their families were primarily responsible for the effectiveness of education; educators were the experts, and schools provided students with the *opportunity* to learn. Students were expected to comply with their educators' demands to acquire knowledge. Schools believed that if parents supported the teacher's expert guidance and encouraged their children to follow that guidance, students would succeed in school. It was not surprising, then, that all students were not academically successful, because levels of support for education were different in every household. Additionally, success or failure in school was determined solely by educators in the form of completely subjective grading scales and procedures controlled exclusively by education professionals. Parents and students had very little recourse if they felt that the system was unfair or was not an accurate appraisal of proficiency or potential.

Conversely, under NCLB and ESSA, the school became exclusively accountable for student success or failure. Results of student performance on state examinations are posted in news publications for public consumption. States have developed evaluation systems for individual school districts and schools, and through this system have assigned ratings ranging from poor to excellent. The real estate industry even started using these test scores as a major factor in determining property values for homes (Chiodo, Hernández-Murillo, & Owyang, 2010). Schools that do not meet the mandated standards have to carry the "failing" label, even though many of them have sincerely fought to overcome barriers outside of the school's control; they have made some progress, but they have not made as much progress as the law mandates. This system of finger-pointing at schools has not motivated people to improve their practice in meaningful ways; instead, it has created anger and resentment among many educators and even more pessimism about the probability of making substantial and permanent change within schools.

I cannot blame educators for feeling unfairly blamed for all of the ills of struggling schools. I do not believe that the old paradigm of exclusively blaming students and parents is just either, but the problem of struggling schools is too complex to hold only the school system accountable for student success. In fact, the Educational Testing Service (ETS) reveals a report that validates the concerns of many educators. The report provides the following explanation for gaps in student achievement:

> The ETS researchers took four variables that are beyond the control of schools: The percentage of children living with one

parent; the percentage of eighth graders absent from school at least three times a month; the percentage of children 5 or younger whose parents read to them daily; and the percentage of eighth graders who watch five or more hours of TV a day. Using just those four variables, the researchers were able to predict each state's results on the federal eighth-grade reading test with impressive accuracy. (Winerip, 2007, p. A7)

Identifying educators as the sole cause of low student performance (or high student performance, for that matter), is not only inaccurate, but it makes the job of developing positive school culture even more difficult. Schools located in areas where risk factors for low achievement are highest are struggling to maintain a good, dedicated workforce of teachers, and negative external critiques and commentary from the public make this difficult job even more challenging and create additional problems that we must address and overcome.

The reform approach of NCLB and ESSA sends the message that schools are *broken*, and they need to be *fixed*. This message sets up a natural conflict. In Finland, the approach is cooperative and integrated, which sends the message to educators that *we need each other* if we hope to get better. I seek to prove in this book that schools don't need to be *fixed*, they need to be *transformed*, and the transformational process is complex.

What About Student Outcomes?

The organizational mechanisms of schools were not designed to judge proficiency based on student outcomes. A look at nearly any teacher-performance evaluation proves that the school, as an organization, has concerned itself with evaluating the effort, process, compliance, and *intentions* of teachers rather than *evidence* of student learning. Decisions about lesson content, student evaluation, and classroom procedures have always been left up to each individual teacher. The leader's ability to create the conditions through which classroom teachers could exercise their autonomous endeavors defined his or her role. Student learning was a result of students' efforts, and, conversely, student failure was a result of students' lack of effort.

The era of accountability has made school systems take an honest look at student outcomes and the conditions that guarantee higher achievement. District leadership has begun to demand information that more accurately and more frequently gives feedback on student performance. Consequently, teachers are challenged to analyze the effectiveness of their classroom instruction in ways that are much more objective than letter grades. What effect has this had on school culture? A focus on meeting mandates and minimum performance indicators has, in many cases, taken focus away from the individual student and his or her holistic development. Many schools are strategizing to avoid embarrassment and public humiliation for not meeting minimum student achievement goals and legislated mandates. I call this phenomenon the *compliance mentality*. This mentality has caused school systems to achieve an acceptable rating by any means necessary, including cheating on tests and excluding students with a high probability of failure on high-stakes assessments.

A Rice University study on the Texas school accountability system and its relationship to student dropout disclosed some startling revelations (Barr, 2008).

- In Texas's public high schools, 135,000 youth drop out prior to graduation every year, resulting in an overall graduation rate of only 33 percent.

- The exit of low-achieving students made it appear as though test scores rose and that the achievement gap between white and minority students was narrowing, which increased ratings.

- There was a correlation between schools' increasing number of dropouts and their rising accountability ratings, suggesting that the accountability system allows principals to retain students deemed at risk of reducing school scores. The study finds that a high proportion of students retained this way will eventually drop out.

These findings are troubling because, according to the study, "The longer such an accountability system governs schools, the more school personnel view students not as children to educate but as potential liabilities or assets for their school's performance indicators, their own careers or their school's funding" (Barr, 2008).

In cases like this one from Texas, the accountability movement actually resulted in the students in need of the most assistance being excluded instead of helped. This certainly was not the legislation's goal. It is important to look at student learning outcomes—but not at the expense of creating a group of disposable students for the purpose of favorable performance ratings.

Predetermination

Like any organization, schools are the sum of their parts. Educators, students, parents, and society as a whole add a component to school that is equally as challenging to deal with as the governmental laws and regulations we have just discussed. The human experience of education plays a major role in how school culture forms and ultimately how well a school operates. The unique human experiences individuals bring into the school are called *predeterminations*. There are three major forms of predetermination: (1) *perceptual*, (2) *intrinsic*, and (3) *institutional*.

Perceptual Predetermination

Perceptual predetermination involves an educator's own socialization and the impact of that socialization on his or her practice in the classroom, including expectations for student performance. Robert L. Green (2005) defines teacher expectations as "inferences that teachers make about the present and future academic achievement and general classroom behavior of their students" (p. 29). Green (2005) goes on to find that these expectations for student success have a two-fold effect in the classroom:

> Teacher expectations affect student achievement primarily in two ways: first, teachers teach more material more effectively and enthusiastically to students for whom they have high expectations; second, teachers respond more favorably to students for whom high expectations are held—in a host of often subtle ways that seem to boost students' expectations for themselves. (p. 29)

So the experiences and perceptions that an educator has before he or she becomes an education professional play a powerful role in how he or she perceives and serves students. Thus, the educator's socialization is as important as his or her professional preparation. Green (2005) points out teachers generally develop positive or negative expectations around the following set of student characteristics: race, gender, social class, disability status, limited English proficiency, student history, physical attractiveness, handwriting, communication, and speech pattern. If educators have developed negative opinions about people in regard to these characteristics, students may start each class period with strikes against them.

We might assume that this problem could be eliminated if a teacher's experience or background was similar to that of his or her students. If the achievement gap is most prevalent in communities with high-minority populations and homes with high poverty, perhaps we should simply hire more teachers with the same backgrounds. Unfortunately, there are not enough certified teachers to fill this demand. A 2015 report from the Shanker Institute finds that Latino and African American students make up nearly 40 percent of American public school students, but only 7.8 percent of American teachers are Latino, and 6.8 percent are African American (Di Carlo, 2015).

Upon further review of the research, we find that the teacher's race and background do not have to be a major factor in forming student expectations. In fact, the research finds that low student expectations cross racial, ethnic, and social class lines. Teachers of similar race and class to their students are just as prone to developing low expectations.

Black students may not be at a disadvantage because of the "mismatch" between student and teacher race. In other words, black teachers are not always more likely to give black students more support and attention than white teachers would, because there may be other factors more powerful in guiding teacher behavior beside race like social class and generational differences. In fact, some black teachers appear to have similarly low expectations for black students as non-black teachers (Ferguson, 1998).

Ron Ferguson (1998) goes on to reveal that this mix of high and low expectations of students among teachers may help explain why poor and minority students fail to gain academic momentum and therefore fall behind students from other groups. A 2015 study of teacher quality in Washington State reveals that the teacher-quality crisis in high-risk schools goes well beyond teacher expectations. The study reveals that for the teachers of students of poverty, as well as African American and Latino students, quality indicators are lower than other teachers in the state of Washington on every measurable category including years of experience and licensure scores (Goldhaber, Lavery, & Theobald, 2015).

In a study done at five of Philadelphia's lowest-performing middle schools, researchers spoke with students to get feedback from them about the kinds of teachers they needed and wanted. The students wanted teachers who were strict but fair, nice and respectful, and who took the time to explain their lessons to them clearly and effectively (Wilson & Corbett, 2001). They wanted teachers who believed in them and taught them in the ways that they learned best. These sound like very reasonable expectations. All these characteristics are cornerstones of a healthy school culture. It is amazing that students have figured out what they need better than the adults in the school and the so-called experts responsible for guiding these professionals.

Teacher expectations clearly play a role in how much students learn, and high expectations can be a very powerful tool if we can create conditions that allow teachers to have a favorable image of students and their ability. This involves the resocializing of those within our schools who have unfavorable expectations of student performance. We must somehow help them replace their existing belief systems with a more informed and accurate assessment of student potential. We will address this issue in chapter 6 (page 77).

Intrinsic Predetermination

Intrinsic predetermination is the student's perception of his or her probability of achieving success in school. The messages students receive from their environment—the home, community, and school—can either build their confidence or work to destroy it. Students who come from homes or communities where high academic achievement is not the norm develop what Ron Ferguson (1998) calls a *self-fulfilling prophecy*. The overwhelming message these students receive says that success in school is not likely. Unfortunately, for students who grow up in communities where poor academic performance is the norm, school becomes a place to hang out until you are old enough to do something else—not a place to prepare for a bright future. In fact, this message is so strong in some communities that students may feel that if they achieve in school, their peers will view them unfavorably. One study of African American students in a very prominent suburb of Cleveland, Ohio, finds that many African American students are afraid of cooperating with teachers and achieving academically because of the risk of being perceived by their fellow African American peers as "acting white" (Ogbu, 2003). This type of cultural resistance to academic excellence makes the job of creating a healthy school culture even more difficult.

There is no doubt that succeeding in school takes hard work and dedication from students. No one can complete a student's assignments for him or her, and no one can take his or her exams. So students need to be immersed in an environment where they are held accountable for studying and completing their assignments, and traditionally, this responsibility falls on the parents. No outside influence is more powerful in a child's life than that of his or her parents. Unfortunately, students who suffer from negative intrinsic predetermination learn many of the self-defeating attitudes and behaviors from their parents. One study sought to measure the difference between the level of cognitive stimulation in poor and middle-class homes by measuring the presence of books, exposure to cultural experiences, and the amount of time parents read or participated in an academic experience with their children—factors that made up what researchers call the HOME (Home Observation Measurement of the Environment) scale (Jencks & Phillips, 1998). The study finds that on the HOME scale of 0–100, black and Latino students scored nine to ten points lower than white students, and socioeconomically disadvantaged homes scored twelve to fifteen points lower than middle-class homes. The study concludes that white students from middle-class homes experience an environment at home that is much like their surroundings at school (Jencks & Phillips, 1998).

For a school to gather the momentum necessary to transform a toxic culture into a healthy one, educators must consider students' intrinsic motivation. It will be hard to raise achievement if students do not care to learn or feel incapable of achieving for various reasons, even if all of the adults in the school believe in them. In this journey to improvement, we must accept the following three realities.

1. Students are the product of their environment, and no one has the ability to choose his or her parents or community.

2. Students' resistance is a product of their experiences. If we are to change this reality, we have to provide them with new and more productive experiences to replace the damaging experiences.

3. Children are not mature enough to understand the ramifications of academic failure; therefore, we cannot leave achievement to student interest alone. In the United States, we require individuals to be age sixteen to drive an automobile, eighteen to vote in an election, and twenty-one to drink alcohol, yet we regularly give children "licenses to fail" at a much younger age when they do not exhibit immediate interest in academics. This is not a good or reasonable practice.

Institutional Predetermination

Even though the U.S. political climate since the end of the 19th century expressed an interest in creating an egalitarian system of education that is dedicated to learning for all students as observed in the test performance mandates of NCLB, I contend that we have institutional barriers in place within the traditional public school system that make that goal very difficult. These policies and procedures are so ingrained within the school system that we often fail to recognize their presence and power.

This system is what Richard DuFour and Robert Eaker (1998) call a *system of sorting*. They suggest that schools were never meant to serve all students; instead, they form a complex system of rules, procedures, and norms with the aim of identifying student proficiency (or lack of proficiency) and tracking students into groups ranging from *remedial* to *gifted*. Our master schedules, staffing allocations, academic policies, and support systems were built on this cognitive separation of students. This system of sorting is inherently unjust, and it depends on a certain level of polarization that will always exclude some students from the full benefit of schooling.

While traveling and consulting with schools across North America and examining course offerings at public schools, especially high schools, I have discovered that academic menus are shaped just like the bell curve. Nearly 10 percent of the classes are for low-performing or special education students, 80 percent of the classes are for "average" or "normal" students, and 10 percent of the courses are made available to those identified as academically gifted. What amazes me is that regardless of location, size, or academic performance, all the schools shared this need to group students in this normal distribution. Even though the tracking issue is most pronounced at the high school level, there is evidence that it starts much earlier (Loveless, 2013). Kindergarten teachers know that students do not all start school at the same academic level. Some students show a much higher readiness level because of prekindergarten exposure to academic content and skills than students who come to school without this exposure. In the early grades, schools usually do not develop systems that physically separate students by academic ability; rather, this separation takes place in a much more informal way within the classroom. This is referred to as *ability grouping*. Students who show greater academic promise also tend to receive special praise and special jobs, and their peers generally view them as the teacher's pet (Jackson, 2011).

By the middle grades, parents begin to become much more vocal in advocating for special classes or labels that identify their children as elite among students. It is not uncommon for parents to demand that their students get special attention and special classes because they are not being challenged in the regular classroom. While serving as a middle school principal for grades 6 to 8, I was told that we needed to create two special course sections for "advanced" students at each grade level.

Each grade level consisted of ten class sections of thirty students each, and each class section was heterogeneously grouped by past academic proficiency. I was basically instructed to isolate two sections of students, sixty students total, at each grade level and give them a label to distinguish them as *academically advanced* in comparison to the other eight class sections, or 240 students, at each grade level. It was never clear what the criteria was for this special designation; I was simply told by central office officials that parents wanted it. I became responsible for creating this pseudo–honors track that would comfortably fit into the limited honors course offerings available in our high schools.

In essence, students spend grades K–8 auditioning for their place within the bell curve. By the time students enter high school, they have already been labeled cognitively disadvantaged, cognitively average, or cognitively advanced. Schools have long operated from the perspective that their responsibility is not to ensure student attainment of predetermined skills, but rather to identify students' natural talents and deficiencies through a standard set of assessments in order to put them in their proper place within the academic continuum. Are we serious about our goal of learning for all students if we maintain a system that thrives on formal and informal tracking?

This bell curve that we see in schools is also a microcosm of the bell curve that we experience in society. In their very controversial book *The Bell Curve: Intelligence and Class Structure in American Life*, Richard Herrnstein and Charles Murray (1994) contend that the gaps between groups that we see in our society along the lines of race, class, gender, and other variables are not socially created, but rather are manifestations of the big difference in cognitive ability as measured through the intelligence quotient (IQ) test. They contend that low IQ, not discrimination or social inequality, is responsible for disparities in income, housing, unemployment, and family structure, among other things. They contend that America has to accept and embrace a group that they call the *cognitive elite*, those people with an IQ above 120. Herrnstein and Murray (1994) are not clear how this cognitive elite group forms, but they provide statistics to make the case that this group is most concentrated among whites and East Asian races.

According to Herrnstein and Murray (1994), we can look at the dynamics of a normal statistical distribution's bell-shaped curve to best understand this. They contend that intelligence divides American society along that distribution; that is, the cognitive elite (very bright) make up about 10 percent of the population, cognitively average people make up 80 percent of the population ranging from bright to normal to dull, and the cognitive underclass (very dull) make up 10 percent of the population as measured by the IQ test. They contend that the position in which people find themselves in society depends most significantly on their natural intelligence. Herrnstein and Murray (1994) also suggest that the public school system's goal of achieving equity in student outcomes is disingenuous and that school systems should focus on how to prepare each student for a "realistic" role in society based on his or her cognitive level.

If we were to accept this argument—if success in school is merely a byproduct of students' natural cognitive talent or lack of talent—we could conclude that school reform is a waste of time. Of course, the work of researchers like Larry Lezotte and Ron Edmonds in identifying the correlates of Effective Schools (Lezotte, 1999), and the evidence Robert J. Marzano presents in *The New Art and Science of Teaching* (Marzano, 2017) and his meta-analysis of effective practice in *What Works in Schools* (Marzano, 2003) are enough to refute this highly suspect argument. In fact, since its publication in 1994, there have been several rebuttals to *The Bell Curve* that prove the authors' assumptions were ill-gotten. But unfortunately, their perspective on how natural intelligence impacts one's success or failure is eerily similar to the structure of today's public schools, where cognitive groupings are rigid and institutionalized. If our goal is to create a community that develops each individual student's talent, we must take an honest look at this institutionalized system of discrimination and segregation and commit to changing it.

A War of Paradigms

The issues facing schools from outside their doors and within their walls certainly present challenges. The interaction of social, economic, parental, and political forces with the experiences and worldviews of educators and students creates a complex school culture that is difficult to transform.

From 2004 to 2007, I conducted formal and informal observations in thirty-four schools across the United States to try to ascertain how the staffs of these schools functioned within their school communities and how their behavior supported or hindered change that could create more favorable conditions for universal student achievement. These schools were in every geographical region of the country. Eleven were elementary schools, fourteen were middle schools, and nine were high schools. (See the appendix on page 157 for specific details about the study design.) My findings shed a powerful light on what we know about toxic school culture, and more important, on how we can overcome staff division and turn around even the most toxic cultures. I believe that if school leaders holistically understand the most important variables in unhealthy learning environments and arm themselves with strategies to uproot and replace the toxic elements, then they can be successful at creating healthy learning environments in their schools.

In my study of these thirty-four schools and how their educators (teachers, counselors, administrators, and support staff) interacted in the school culture and articulated their beliefs through their behavior, I found a war of belief systems. I found four distinct groups, two of which were actively engaged in a battle to make their belief system the norm of the school. Each of these two groups had distinct characteristics and "weapons" (behaviors and tools) that it used to exercise its will. A third group found itself in the center of the battle, and a fourth group just tried to survive the school day. These four groups and their characteristics had a divisive impact on the school culture. I determined that in order to transform from a toxic to a healthy learning environment, it is essential for leaders to understand and influence change within these groups of educators inside the school.

- **Believers:** The first group I identified is the Believers. Believers are educators who believe in the core values that make up a healthy school culture. They believe that all of their students are capable of learning and that they have a direct impact on student success. They are actively engaged in a constant battle of ideas with another group, the Fundamentalists.

- **Tweeners:** The second group I call the Tweeners. Tweeners are educators who are new to the school culture. Their experience can be likened to a "honeymoon period" in which they spend time trying to learn the norms and expectations of the school's culture. They end up in the middle of the war of ideas between the Believers and Fundamentalists.

- **Survivors:** The third group I identify is the Survivors. Fortunately, this group is not widespread in our schools. They are the small group of teachers who are burned out— so overwhelmed by the profession's demands that they suffer from depression and merely survive from day to day. This group is much smaller in number than the other groups, and there is a general consensus from all groups that education is not the best profession for them.

- **Fundamentalists:** The fourth group I call the Fundamentalists. Fundamentalists are staff members who are not only opposed to change but organize to resist and thwart any change initiative. They can wield tremendous political power and are a major obstacle in implementing meaningful school reform. They actively work against the Believers.

Table 2.1 shows each classification of educator and its goals. Believers believe in academic success for each student. Tweeners believe in organizational stability. Survivors are concerned with their own emotional and mental survival, and Fundamentalists want to maintain the status quo.

Table 2.1: The Four Types of Educators and Their Goals

Educator Classification	Organizational Goal
Believer	Academic success for each student
Tweener	Organizational stability
Survivor	Emotional and mental survival
Fundamentalist	Maintaining the status quo

In the following chapters, I will identify the distinct characteristics of each group and describe how they form, behave, and interact with the school system, students, and one another to create a distinct and divided school culture.

CHAPTER 3

The Believers

We have already learned that there is a high correlation between teacher expectations and student performance. During my study of school culture, one group emerged that possessed the ability to achieve higher levels of student performance and satisfaction in the classroom as compared to its colleagues. Its actions manifested its commitment to student success. This group was composed of seasoned educators (practicing more than three years) who had made a decision to accept a student-centered paradigm as their primary mode of operation, regardless of outside opposition. I call this group the Believers.

I found Believers in every school I visited. Their number and level of influence varied from school to school, but their presence was definitely felt on each campus. It did not matter if the school was high or low performing; each had a set of Believers who fought in many different ways for an ideal learning environment.

Jocelyn A. Butler and Kate M. Dickson's (1987) study on transformational school cultures identifies twelve characteristics of powerful and positive school cultures.

1. Collegiality

2. Experimentation

3. High expectations

4. Trust and confidence

5. Tangible support

6. Reaching out to the knowledge bases

7. Appreciation and recognition

8. Caring, celebration, and humor

9. Involvement in decision making

10. Protection of what is important

11. Honoring traditions

12. Honest, open communication

I found similar characteristics and aspirations in the Believers I studied. In their journey to establish a healthy school culture, the Believers encountered resistance. Others in the school had very different goals and worked to suppress the characteristics of positive and powerful school culture. The intensity of this clash of values became a factor in how effective Believers were within their school culture. Their intrinsic paradigm coupled with outside influences created a set of very noticeable characteristics. These characteristics include:

- High levels of intrinsic motivation
- Personal connection to the school and community
- High levels of flexibility with students
- Application of positive student pressure
- Willingness to confront opposing viewpoints
- Varied levels of pedagogical skills

The Believers' ultimate goal was success for every student academically, socially, and emotionally. They were not happy and they did not feel successful unless every student within their influence maximized his or her potential. They worked with all other willing stakeholders in multiple arenas to accomplish this goal. They had a strong presence on school-improvement teams, curriculum initiatives, and voluntary committees. Change was not foreign and threatening to them; in fact, they embraced any change that they felt would improve student performance.

Intrinsic Motivation

During interviews with building principals, I asked the following question: "If you were to start an initiative that provided an extra benefit for students but required teachers to work outside of the contractual day, which staff members could you count on to participate?" Without exception, each principal's answer correlated by at least 90 percent with my findings: they named the same staff members whom I had already identified as Believers. Believers demonstrated a willingness to put forth more than the required effort. They made themselves available and in many cases sought opportunities to contribute to any effort that they viewed as positively affecting students.

Believers appeared to have a consistency and drive that did not depend on the influence of leadership. In the schools I observed, although teacher perception of administrator effectiveness ranged widely from *extremely low* to *exceptional*, the observable characteristics of the Believers remained the same, regardless of the quality of their leadership. Many of the schools that I studied were known publicly as low performing or failing, but these labels and public perception did not seem to deter the Believers. In fact, there was no detectable difference in performance between Believers in schools labeled high performing and those labeled low performing. These indicators reveal a high level of personal commitment to education and the goals of an egalitarian educational system on the part of the Believers.

There were also several other indicators of a high level of intrinsic motivation among the Believers. One that is very telling is also very basic: work attendance. When reviewing the attendance records of the educators I observed, I found a significant disparity in days away from work between the Believers and other groups. In fact, Believers appear to understand what many researchers are just beginning to grasp: inconsistency and frequent changes in instructors greatly impact student achievement. A Duke University study finds that in North Carolina, for every ten days of absence of a first- or second-year teacher, a student's reading and mathematics test scores in fourth and fifth grade decline by about one-fifth the advantage of a first- or second-year teacher with less than five days of absence (Keller, 2008). The study goes on to find:

Schools with high proportions of poor children suffered more from teacher absences. For instance, the poorest 25 percent of schools averaged almost one more sick day per teacher than the richest 25 percent. And schools with persistently high rates of teacher sick and personal days were more likely to serve low-income than high-income students. (p. 1)

Believer attendance was solid in every school examined in this study, and external variables like location, ethnicity of students, the community's socioeconomic profile, and personal profile of the Believer did not serve as a deterrent to solid work attendance.

Other indicators of intrinsic commitment and motivation included attendance at voluntary professional development opportunities, membership in professional organizations, and a willingness to purchase classroom materials with personal funds.

Connection to the School and Community

Another area of distinction for Believers was their life pattern. Demographic data on the participants revealed a clear pattern of home ownership within reasonable proximity to the school. Only 10 percent of the Believers in this study rented their residence or had an unstable housing situation. The home ownership variable reveals that the Believers made a conscious decision to build their lives in close proximity to their work environment, which indicates that they plan to continue their employment and participation at their school for some time to come.

Many Believers that I interviewed indicated that they met their spouse in the community in which they live and work and that their children either attended the district of their employment or a neighboring district. Their religious and civic alliances were also built in close proximity to their home and work environments, further solidifying their ties to the school community.

This commitment to their profession and individual schools brought Believers a sense of stability and appeared to shape their relationships with students in a positive way; they shared a community with them. During classroom observations, students would regularly talk about seeing their teacher at the grocery store or at church. This sense of familiarity seemed to produce a positive bond between students and educators.

Flexibility

Of all the characteristics of Believers, none was more striking than the high level of flexibility they demonstrated. While other educators were very strict with school rules, grading procedures, seating arrangements, and other similar issues, Believers sought to individualize their responses to students instead of adopting a rigid approach to student relations. It was clear that the main goal of the Believers—student success—motivated their desire to be flexible. In one seventh-grade science classroom I observed, students lined up at the teacher's desk to turn in a science project. The class had been working on the project for over six weeks, and students' grades on the project would constitute more than 50 percent of their final grade for the marking period. As students lined up, one young lady still sat with her arms folded on her desk and her head resting on her arms. When she finally lifted her head, it was apparent she had been crying. After all the projects had been turned in, the teacher—a Believer—noticed the student's posture, tapped her, and asked the student to follow her into the hall so that they could talk. When they returned, the expression on the student's face and her entire disposition had changed dramatically. She was smiling, and the anxiety she displayed earlier seemed to have dissipated.

After the students were released from class, I approached the teacher to inquire about her actions in the hall and the source of the student's anxiety. The teacher explained that this student was very conscientious and had never missed a deadline for turning in an assignment. She went on to explain that the student's parents were going through a painful divorce, and the combativeness of her parents sometimes caused her to be displaced with relatives. The previous evening, the teacher explained, the student's father was intoxicated and tried to force his way into their home. Her mother called the police, and her father was arrested. Consequently, the student spent the evening at her aunt's home. Her science project was at her dad's apartment, and the student did not know if she could return to get it any time soon.

The teacher extended the deadline for the student, and she informed her that she would share the details of her situation with the principal so they could contact the grandfather to see if he would be willing to drop the project off at school. The teacher followed through with her promise, and before the day was over, the girl's grandfather delivered her project to the school.

In this situation, the teacher chose to talk to the student before drawing a conclusion about her anxiety and penalizing her for the lateness of the very important assignment. When I asked the teacher about her flexible and personalized approach to the situation, she replied, "I want these kids to learn and love science. I do not care about rules or deadlines. I want to spark something special in my students, and if bending a little does the trick, that is a small price to pay."

Believers also showed flexibility in their classroom management and in their interpretation of the student code of conduct. When reviewing school discipline data, Believers wrote formal discipline referrals to the office at nearly 30 percent the rate of Fundamentalists. Was it that the Believers did not encounter student discipline issues? The answer is no; they, too, encountered difficult students. What differed were the methods they used to manage discipline incidents. These methods were rooted in intentions that differed significantly from those of other groups in the school.

Believers generally had high expectations for student conduct, but they chose to use nonpunitive measures more often than punitive measures. When behavior issues arose, they relied heavily on student loyalty, which they gained through positive personal relationships. Students seemed to lament the fact that they disappointed an advocate instead of rejoicing over whatever personal pleasure they gained through the conduct violation.

Believers used observable classroom management techniques at a much higher rate than other groups within the school. Many of these techniques were informal and private. A significant number of Believers had a "look" that communicated seriousness to a student who was violating a rule. This had an immediate impact on the student that other teachers, even after writing disciplinary referrals and threatening punishment, could not achieve. The authors of *Listening to Urban Kids: School Reform and the Teachers They Want* find that the students they studied in urban Philadelphia schools really admired and respected teachers who "stayed on them" and "made them be successful" (Wilson & Corbett, 2001, p. 73). Teacher efficacy is one of the most influential factors in creating an environment of student growth. Students observe the formal and informal cues of the teacher, and they are very adept at identifying if a teacher has a deep interest in their success (Jones, Bouffard, & Weissbourd, 2013). Students in these schools had a very low level of respect for teachers who wrote a lot of referrals; they considered them to be "weak" and "scared" (Wilson & Corbett, 2001, p. 71). Students in the Believers' classrooms displayed a high level of respect for their teachers. They knew these teachers believed strongly in students' ability to not only achieve academically but also behaviorally. And they knew their teachers understood that they would make mistakes at times. There was an understanding that most issues would be resolved in the classroom, and the main office was reserved for serious issues or severe problems.

Positive Pressure

Believers do not want to see any student fail. This desire produces a very observable characteristic called *positive pressure*. Positive pressure is a collection of unrelenting responses to student underperformance and apathy. The teacher simply does not allow the student to fail. In the classrooms of Believers I observed, it was apparent that to students, failure was not a possibility. Even students who were not performing well in other classes met at least minimum learning standards in Believers' classrooms.

Strategies for positive pressure took many forms, including calling parents, moving a student's seat closer to the teacher, detaining students from lunch or recess socialization, providing positive incentives, and requiring after-school tutoring, to name a few. If one strategy did not produce the breakthrough that the Believer expected, he or she tried a new one and repeated this process until the student met the classroom academic and behavioral expectations. Some Believers used a stoic and very strict approach in their pressure, and others took a motivational approach similar to a football coach firing the team up before the biggest game of the season. Their methods varied, but the end result consistently indicated that the student understood that failure was not an option in the classroom and that resistance only brought on a new wave of pressure.

It was very apparent that Believers felt every student was capable of learning the assigned curriculum. Believers did not have different performance expectations for each student. The evidence is very clear that varying student expectations based on unscientific observation has a real effect on student performance:

> In his 1983 review of the teacher expectations research, Jere Brophy estimated that five to ten percent of the variance in student performance is attributable to differential treatment accorded them based on their teachers' differential expectations of them. Various other researchers have accepted and quoted this estimate. Five to ten percent is hardly the epidemic of mistreatment and negative outcomes perceived by some educators and members of the general public, but it is significant enough, particularly when compounded through year after year of schooling, to warrant concern. (Cotton, 1989, p. 11)

This unwavering expectation of universal student achievement was the driving force behind all of the positive pressure. Teacher expectations affect more than just an individual student; they can affect an entire class. Christine Rubie-Davies (2006) analyzed the development of 256 students who were exposed to teachers who had either high or low expectations of student performance at the beginning of the school year. She reassessed the same students at the end of the school year and added a sub-scale to assess the students' opinion about their teacher's confidence in their academic ability. The study shows that classes with a low-expectation teacher collectively lost academic confidence, and their performance gradually declined by the end of the school year, while classes with a high-expectation teacher experienced a greater sense of self-confidence and academic performance (Rubie-Davies, 2006).

In a ninth-grade science class, a young man entered the classroom, put his head on the desk, and withdrew from class participation before the class had even officially begun. His teacher approached him and whispered in his ear. I guessed that he was giving the student gentle verbal encouragement to participate with the class. The student did not respond. About two minutes later, the teacher approached the student again and told the whole class how much he really wanted the disinterested student to come to the front and help him demonstrate an experiment. This attempt caused the student to lift his head for a moment and make eye contact with the teacher, but he still did not speak or move to participate. On the third attempt, the teacher stated to the class that the disinterested student was a scientific whiz kid and his great performance during last week's football game proved how well he solved problems and that he was best qualified to demonstrate this experiment. The teacher expressed to the class that "the best" was the only acceptable option in his class and that the class would not continue until the disinterested student assisted with the demonstration. This caused many of the more involved and interested students to verbally coerce the student into participating. As he approached the teacher, the student mumbled his displeasure, but the peer pressure had cracked his aloof disposition, and he complied with the teacher's command to participate for the rest of the class period.

After the class ended, I asked the teacher how often he used similar techniques with this student. He told me about once per week, but during the first three weeks of school he had to use them daily. The student was currently earning a C in his class, and he had never before passed a science class since entering secondary school. The teacher further explained that failure is not allowed in his class, and that rule is nonnegotiable. He expressed that he would use every available means to enforce this rule.

Willingness to Confront

Many of the attributes of Believers—such as high expectations for student behavior and achievement, effective connection with students, patience, and flexibility—reflect best practice as supported by the research on improving student performance. It would seem, then, that Believers would aggressively recruit others to these ideas; however, this was not the case in the classrooms I studied. In fact, Believers tended to speak out and challenge others only when something overtly intolerant was exhibited. Believers, as a whole, appeared to be passive and permissive of others where issues of inequity, low student expectations, and roadblocks to school reform were concerned, except in extreme cases.

In one staff meeting I observed in a rural middle school, the principal delivered a presentation on the latest student test results from the state's standardized test. The news was not good. Not only did student performance not improve, it actually got worse. As the meeting went on, it was apparent that all were displeased they had missed their federal achievement goal of adequate yearly progress (AYP) for the third straight year. One staff member raised his hand as the principal finished explaining all of the details of the assessment results and said, "We never had this problem before they built that trailer park around the corner." Immediately, two Believers scolded him for his comments. I only observed Believers speaking out or challenging viewpoints in similar extreme circumstances. When their peers exhibited similar beliefs through much more subtle means, such as in casual comments about student potential, general complaints about school or district function, or consistent pessimism about the school-improvement process, Believers were silent. They appeared to be content to work with their students and control their own spheres of influence instead of actively engaging their colleagues in philosophical debates about what they felt was best for students.

If schools are going to effectively create positive and productive cultures, the Believers simply have to become more active and aware of the day-to-day assaults on the very belief system that they adhere to. They have strong cases for their stance: research and ethics support their goal of success for every student. If Believers would simply engage in intellectual discourse on a regular and consistent basis, they might discover that they could change school culture for the better beyond their own spheres.

Human beings have a natural fear of conflict (Patterson, Grenny, McMillan, & Switzler, 2002, 2012), and this was definitely the case with Believers, who often chose the *flight* response over their *fight* response. Educators tend to have a hard time stimulating the courage necessary to challenge the behavior or belief systems of a colleague. It has not been a part of our history, and most Believers that I interviewed felt that it was *inappropriate*. I want to challenge Believers to work against that instinct and choose to engage with opposition as opposed to withdrawing. I am not encouraging a civil war or a heated battle of words, I am simply advocating for a balance of ideas. If educators who have become self-centered and comfortable with the status quo (Fundamentalists) feel comfortable with voicing their opinions, even when unsolicited, why can't the Believer? Everyone is entitled to his or her opinion, but the problem with school culture is that the Believer's opinion is often absent during the philosophical exchange of ideas in most schools. When Believers learn the power of their ideas and develop the courage to speak up in all situations, they will unleash a powerful wave of positive peer pressure.

Peer pressure is a very powerful influencer of human behavior. A 2013 study proves that appealing to a person's desire for a good reputation is more powerful than money or any other extrinsic motivator (Yoeli, Hoffman, Rand, & Nowak, 2013). Positive peer pressure forces a peer to engage at a high moral level. Believers do not have to argue, scream, or defame others; their power is in the morality of their intentions. In my research, I observed positive peer pressure being levied with simple, but loaded, questions like:

- "That's interesting, but how does that help us move closer to our goal?"

- "I'm struggling to see your point; could you help me understand how this idea is better for students?"

- "I respect your opinion, but can you accept that everyone does not see it the same way that you do?"

- "Do you mind if we stay focused on the task at hand, because I am uncomfortable with talking about the intentions of colleagues who are not present?"

I discovered that the schools with healthy cultures tended to be populated with Believers who were willing to defend their moral and professional objectives. As we'll see, Fundamentalists had a hard time going *low* in an environment where Believers stayed *high*. If Believers truly want to improve their impact, they have to become less concerned about being favorable in the eyes of Fundamentalists and more concerned about remaining true to themselves and the students that they serve.

Pedagogical Skill

The Believers' paradigm was very consistent: all students must be successful. But there were huge variances in the level of teaching skill Believers exhibited. In many cases, I observed Believers who not only held to the principle that all students can learn but they employed teaching methodologies that best promoted achieving that goal. In these classrooms, I saw many instances of effective use of instructional technology, cooperative learning activities, differentiation for student learning style, and ongoing formative assessment with immediate feedback for students. These methods coupled with the teachers' belief systems made Believers' classrooms havens for student performance.

Unfortunately, in many other classrooms, I observed similar paradigms with pedagogy that perpetuated gaps in student achievement. Simply put, many Believers wanted all their students to learn at high levels, but they did not know how to make that desire a reality. In many cases, I observed all of the character attributes of a Believer coupled with methods like silent reading, hour-long lectures, photocopied worksheets, and low-level question-and-answer sessions. It was apparent that the teachers who used these methods were affected by their students' lack of growth, but they were clueless to the fact that their methodology was the key variable in that lack of growth.

In order to close the achievement gap, we need to do more than just believe in our students; we need to properly instruct and guide them. Our field has a wealth of available research on the most effective teaching methods for each student enrolled in our public school system. Educators who adopt egalitarian idealism as the center of their educational paradigm must cultivate professionalism as well. In order to achieve an end, a person must have conviction, but that conviction must be buttressed with skill.

A Unifying Force

Believers display the qualities and value the paradigms that unite staff members and make a positive school culture. Their core beliefs are in alignment with the schools' stated mission: success for every student. They have high expectations for student achievement, and they are willing to embrace strategies that improve their performance. They have made a commitment, not only to the field but also to the communities that they serve. If schools are to transform their cultures into fertile ground for positive experimentation and student nurturing, they must increase their population of Believers, and their Believers must become more vocal members of the school community.

CHAPTER 4

The Tweeners

A Tweener is anyone who is new to a particular culture. The most common Tweeners in the schools I observed were new educators who had recently graduated from college and were experiencing their first teaching jobs, and, less frequently, educators who had chosen teaching as a second career. I call brand-new educators *Level One Tweeners*; they made up 91 percent of the educators identified in the Tweener category in this study. But an experienced educator who moves into a new school, district, or job categorization is also a Tweener. I refer to these educators as *Level Two Tweeners*; because their introduction and socialization into their new environment do not have nearly the impact on school culture as the Level Ones, they are not the focus of this chapter.

My study revealed that a new educator, a Level One Tweener, has an introductory period of two to four years. A Level Two Tweener (one who changes work environments within the field of education) has a shorter introductory period of one to two years. This introductory period is unpredictable. What happens then can shape the career of these educators and the school environments in which they work. Therefore, a Tweener's primary goal is to find stability within the organization and understand how he or she fits within its cultural and political goals. In this chapter, I'll discuss Tweeners in regard to:

1. A loose connection with the school and community

2. An enthusiastic nature in regard to their students, school, community, and nation

3. A disposition of compliance as part of the "honeymoon period"

4. High attrition rates

A Loose Connection

One very easily observable characteristic of the Tweeners, especially the first-time educators, was their very loose connection with the school and community. Simply put, they did not have a lot at stake within the organization. Their employment contract or employment agreement created their connection, and that relationship could be broken easily.

Unlike the Believers, the Tweeners had a very low level of home ownership. Of the Tweeners studied, 92 percent identified themselves as renters, and more than 70 percent had at least one roommate who was not a relative. This is significant because home ownership creates a natural bond with a city or region. It is a major step in establishing roots. This characteristic makes the Tweeners huge flight risks. They have not made the financial commitments that symbolize stability and longevity.

Because the vast majority of Level One Tweeners are recent college graduates, it should not be surprising that the median age was twenty-four. It should also not be surprising that only 9 percent had children, and 18 percent were married. These two factors also create bonds to a city or a region that could promote longevity within the school system.

Tweeners' loose coupling with the organization makes leaving a viable choice at all times. The bonds that prevent mobility are simply not present for them. If schools are going to develop their cultures, they must take this fact into serious consideration. Administrators must do more than simply hire people with attractive resumes and hope that they stay and become positive contributors to the staff.

School leaders can strengthen these loose bonds by intentionally creating strong bonds in other areas. As I interviewed Tweeners, I asked them about their personal lives, and they were more than happy to share details with me. Many expressed affinity for sports, the arts, religion, community service, and a host of other interests. When I asked if their administrators had inquired about their personal interests, I heard a nearly unanimous "no." Tweeners' personal interests can be a powerful link in the quest to retain these new educators in our schools.

Intentionally placing these new professionals in key positions within our schools that connect with their areas of personal interest can create a bond with the school that may not occur otherwise. These bonds help Tweeners navigate the sometimes-tumultuous early years in the classroom and create the positive experiences necessary for them to align their paradigms with those of the Believers.

Strengthening the bond of Tweeners is absolutely crucial to developing positive school culture. A 2014 study reports that 41 percent of new teachers who enter the educational profession leave the field before their fifth year in the classroom. Nearly 45 percent of the total turnover can be attributed to only one-quarter of all new teachers; schools where more than half of the students are poor or minority (Ingersoll, Merrill, & Stuckey, 2014). How can schools improve if they lose half of their new practitioners before their fifth year of practice? This creates constant turnover in the classroom, which studies have indicated hinders the academic progress of students (Barnes, Schaefer, & Crowe, 2007).

More important, schools simply cannot gather the momentum necessary to create change over the long term because they lack *organizational memory*—the momentum carried from year to year by an organization's members. This phenomenon is very observable in the world of team sports. Teams that build a core group of players who grow and develop together and take positive steps toward winning a championship carry the team goals and norms with them from year to year. An athlete who joins that team is quickly introduced to the norms, values, and goals of that team, and key members of the team force compliance with their influence. On the flip side, if a team's roster of athletes and coaches changes from year to year and no clear nucleus is established, that team usually flounders and struggles to search for an identity. Consequently, victories become rare as the team grows more and more unstable. Schools are no different. Unless the school achieves positive stability through a large coalition of its members, it is incapable of sustaining growth over time. If membership constantly turns over, training and professional initiatives have no long-term effectiveness. School districts that are serious about growth and reform must be proactive in their plans to strengthen the bond between the school and the Tweener.

An Enthusiastic Nature

Tweeners are enthusiastic about what they can contribute to their students, school, community, and nation through their service in the classroom. Interviews with new teachers clearly reveal that they do not become educators because they seek financial wealth. A National Education Association (NEA) report on motivating and retaining new teachers finds that new teachers seek the profession for intrinsic satisfaction as opposed to financial gain (Kopkowski, 2008). Indeed, teachers' starting salaries are much lower than many other professions.

The Tweeners I studied cited many reasons for their career choice. Many said that a teacher inspired them during their own K–12 schooling experience and they wanted to provide that same inspiration for others. Nearly 20 percent of those interviewed indicated that at least one of their parents was an educator and he or she wanted to follow the same career path. Several Tweeners described some religious conviction that called them into service through the classroom. A significant number of Tweeners simply indicated that they wanted to serve humanity and give back to society. The reasons may have varied, but it was clear that Tweeners chose the field of education because they felt they could make a positive impact on society.

This willingness to serve takes many forms in the beginning stages of a teaching career. Tweeners tried to immerse themselves in their new culture by participating in voluntary committees, attending staff social functions, and arriving at the school site early and leaving late. Tweeners, especially in the beginning stages, seized every opportunity to learn about their new environment.

This enthusiasm was evident in the classroom as well, especially when it came to the aesthetic quality of the classroom, which reflected a focus on theme and decoration and what Tweeners learned during their time in college methods courses. The classroom of the typical Tweener seemed to be a monument to his or her subject matter and the students he or she served. Additionally, there was very clear evidence of recent research-based pedagogical methods, which also directly reflected their recent status as college students. Lessons that took into account student learning style or multiple intelligence research were not uncommon.

The Tweeners were typically not afraid to experiment and try a wide variety of methods in the classroom.

Tweeners also appeared to be very enthusiastic about achieving universal academic proficiency within their classrooms. When asked about barriers to learning like poverty, minimal parental involvement, and attendance, the typical Tweener believed that he or she could overcome one or all of these obstacles. They were honest enough to admit that they did not know exactly how to achieve this reality, but they felt that with hard work and perseverance, they and their students could overcome these factors. In essence, they believed that all of their students could learn at high levels, but they were not quite sure how to accomplish that end.

The "Honeymoon Period" and Compliance

Approaching any new situation can cause a person to become cautious and reluctant to reveal his or her faults—both perceived and real—to others. Tweeners are no different. Because they are new to the school culture, they often display reluctance to being viewed unfavorably by their new peers. This is a natural phenomenon. There is no person that the Tweener wants to impress more than his or her supervisor, primarily the school principal. This person has the power to determine whether or not the new educator continues his or her employment with the school or district, and in some cases whether he or she stays in the field. School administrators have the tremendous power of evaluation, which can be intimidating—especially to someone who is simply trying to find comfort and stability within an organization. Tweeners in the study generally displayed a high level of reverence—sometimes bordering on fear—for their school and district supervisors.

This fear and uncertainty caused an observable obsession among Tweeners for pleasing a supervisor, primarily through compliance with directives. Whenever Tweeners were given orders, they complied. In the Tweeners' mind, missing a deadline or ignoring a directive could mean displeasing the principal and in turn threaten their livelihood within the profession. Tweeners hoped that compliance with directives would articulate to administrators that they were team players, and that in return administrators would reward them with a favorable evaluation.

During my interviews, I asked principals their opinions of certain teachers. I knew how I had categorized those teachers, but the principals did not. Time after time, the administrator identified the Tweener teacher as a "good teacher." When I probed and asked for evidence of proficiency, the principals expressed that these good teachers were compliant and cooperative, had high levels of collegiality, and were politically neutral. There was rarely any evidence given relating to their proficiency in the most important aspect of the schooling: student learning. Principals were pleased that the Tweeners followed directions and complied with mandates—but are these the criteria for good professional practice in today's environment? Today's school leaders have to be concerned with issues far more important than management tasks and compliance with mandates. I call the communication barrier between the Tweener and school leader *The Wall of Silence*. The Tweener's desire to please and appear competent, coupled with the leader's desire to lead a congenial and compliant staff, means that critical revelations about the Tweener's true needs may be missed.

An overwhelming body of evidence proves that highly effective schools have school leaders who are strong *instructional* leaders (DuFour & Marzano, 2011). These leaders are involved in critical decisions about what students learn and how students are assessed, and they help develop support systems that ensure high levels of learning for all students. This type of leader is especially necessary in the current era of academic accountability.

This very surface-level look at teacher performance blinded some administrators to hidden problems. Though Tweeners displayed an enthusiastic disposition in public, many of them suffered from the trials of learning to master their craft. Foundational tasks and issues such as classroom management, implementation of curriculum, administrative paperwork, and the fast pace of school make the first few years of teaching difficult (Allen, 2005). How could a Tweener balance the need to please the administrator and at the same time seek support for the many struggles experienced within the first few years in the profession? The balance is very difficult to strike. Administrators often assume everything is running smoothly because of the Tweener's high level of compliance and sunny disposition, but the teacher may be experiencing significant difficulty and trials. This causes some Tweeners, especially the ones who struggle severely in their first few years in the profession, to live in two worlds: (1) a private world of struggle and doubt, and (2) a public world of false enthusiasm and positivity. These two worlds are on a collision course to what I call the *moment of truth*.

The moment of truth is the very critical moment when an educator questions his or her likelihood of continuing in the field. Any experienced educator remembers that moment well and the conditions that caused it. The reasons can vary from an explosive confrontation with parents to an unresponsive student who refuses to comply with classroom rules and regulations. No matter what the circumstances, this very painful moment is significant in an educator's career. It is the first time the educator seriously questions whether he or she will continue or consider other career options. I am sure there are similar moments in any career, but for educators, who very often choose education in order to serve the common good, this moment can be especially painful.

In one very vivid example, I observed a young middle school science teacher who appeared to have all of the necessary attributes to evolve into being a very solid educator. During my initial observations, she displayed the trademark enthusiasm and willingness to serve that are typical of a Tweener. I observed her in her classroom, which showed all the evidence of her recent college courses and the teaching methods she used with her students.

I returned to the same school the following fall, nearly a year later, and her entire disposition had changed. She appeared personally and professionally withdrawn, combative with students, and generally pessimistic about the direction of the school. I approached her principal after the second observation and inquired about the drastic change in her behavior. He informed me that she had a very traumatic experience in the middle of the previous school year from which she had not yet recovered. She had a disagreement with a student about a grade the student received on a very important classroom project. After being unable to convince the teacher that her grade should be changed, the student went to the restroom to call her mother from her cell phone.

The student returned to class, and the teacher continued to teach. Shortly after the student returned to class, her mother appeared in the classroom and confronted the teacher, hurling profanity and insulting comments until the teacher began to cry. Some of the students showed support for their teacher, while others laughed at her misfortune. This became her crucial moment of truth.

A critical event such as this in the career of a Tweener signifies prime recruitment time for Fundamentalists (discussed in detail in chapter 6 on page 77). Fundamentalists displayed a consistent pattern of refraining from heavily influencing Tweeners until they had personally experienced an unexpected disruption to their development. This technique proved to be very savvy and effective. Fundamentalists greatly increased their likelihood of success at selling their political stance while the Tweener was in a weak or vulnerable moment. The strategy was to teach the Tweener how to survive and maintain sanity by isolating him- or herself from the other parts or members of the school. They convinced the Tweener that belonging to the brotherhood of educators who had also been through a critical experience and survived was essential to longevity in the field. Their words and outward show of empathy provided the Tweener with a sense of comfort, and later the Tweener started to share many more job frustrations, causing the new educator to eventually become a Fundamentalist. I observed this pattern repeatedly in many different schools and circumstances. How could this have been avoided? It could've been avoided in three ways.

1. **Site and district administrators must realize that new educators will struggle in the early phases of practice:** Tweeners need to know that those in leadership positions support them and are not only willing to listen to their struggles, but also will be a partner in resolving those struggles.

2. **Administrators must establish and institutionalize proper and ongoing mentorship:** The Tweener needs to be connected with a stellar example of professionalism and have access to that mentor on a regular basis.

3. **School leadership must methodically work to connect the new educator to the school community:** This can be done effectively through making an immediate and positive connection with the Tweener—by taking advantage of the gifts and talents he or she brings to the school. This personal connection will increase the likelihood that the new educator will have a vested interest in the school and that negative experiences will be counteracted with a series of positive experiences to help the new teacher weather the storm of the moment of truth.

Tweener Attrition

If public schools are to improve, the Tweeners must be secured and vested in the long-term future of our system. Every year, many of our best and brightest college students graduate and enter the ranks of the teaching profession. The problem is that they do not stay.

The NEA describes the problem like this:

> Their departure [new teachers] through what researchers call the "revolving door" that's spinning ever faster . . . costs roughly $7 billion a year, as districts and states recruit, hire, and try to retain new teachers. "There is this idea that we can solve the teaching shortage with recruitment," says commission President Tom Carroll. "What we have is a retention crisis." Likening it to continually dumping sand into a bucket with holes in the bottom, Carroll says, "as fast as [the districts] are moving teachers into schools, they're leaving." (as cited in Kopkowski, 2008, p. 2)

There has been a slight break in the trend of teachers leaving the profession in increasing numbers, but the underlying causes of the retention are very disturbing. For example, NCES's teacher follow-up surveys reveal that the number of new teachers leaving the profession between 2007 and 2013 actually declined (Di Carlo, 2015). This defies conventional wisdom, because most experts predicted that external expectations to improve from NCLB would frustrate more teachers into leaving the profession, especially new teachers (Hill &

Barth, 2004). However, the teacher follow-up survey (Di Carlo, 2015) notes three disturbing reasons for the decline in new teacher turnover.

1. The Great Recession that the housing crash in the U.S. market caused created a tight job market, and many new teachers did not leave the profession because of the bleak employment prospects in the open job market. Most teachers reported very low job satisfaction, but chose to stay to preserve their income, not because of workplace satisfaction.

2. There was no decrease in the turnover of teachers who served highly economically disadvantaged students. The rate of attrition was twice that of teachers working in economically affluent areas.

3. Because of tight state and federal budgets, due to the Great Recession, many states like North Carolina and Ohio raised their minimum age for retirement. More veteran teachers, who would have considered retiring in a better economic climate, chose to stay longer than they planned, which created fewer job opportunities for new teachers.

If schools, especially those serving the lowest-achieving groups, fail to retain new practitioners, the progress that we hope to achieve in public schools is highly unlikely and probably impossible to achieve. If the poorest and neediest students are consistently guided by novice professionals who never evolve into proficient instructors, they will constantly be behind.

The transition from NCLB to ESSA may potentially introduce some positive news for teachers, especially new teachers. Since the ESSA provides much more autonomy to states to prescribe their own path for school improvement compared to NCLB, there is an opportunity for states to change the trajectory of the American school system. States like Wyoming, Delaware, Georgia, and Arkansas are embracing the PLC at Work model as a framework for school reform and investing in training and professional support. This opportunity would place Tweeners in a collaborative culture that supports their growth and development and provides them with access to support from their colleagues and school administration that would mitigate some of the damage of isolation (DuFour, 2016). These states have provided leadership, and they have the opportunity to provide a blueprint for other states on holistic school reform that builds culture rather than destroys it.

Tweeners are important for two major reasons: first, as noted in the previous chapter, a school cannot gain momentum if it lacks organizational memory. Members of an organization who are connected to a long-term plan for improvement and participate in that improvement incrementally over time carry with them the experiences, training, and expertise necessary to make that long-term vision a reality. This type of long-range continuity is not possible if the members of an organization consistently change and initiatives have to be revamped or scrapped because knowledge and experience are lost through a revolving door. New members then enter the organization clueless about the past attempts to improve the organization and the organizational vision. Organizations with no memory simply survive; they never reach a point where they can thrive. America's schools cannot make long-term progress if they replace 50 percent of their professional staff every five years.

Tweeners are also important to the evolution of a school and its culture because they present the best opportunity for the growth of the Believers. Administrators can look at schools with a very high number of inexperienced teachers as either a crisis or an opportunity. We must remember that Tweeners are trying to find stability and meaning; they are blank slates. Administrators who provide these new professionals with proper support can fill that slate with good experiences and drastically change the school culture.

The National Staff Development Council (NSDC), now Learning Forward, agrees, and it makes the following recommendations:

> Teachers—even those in the most demanding settings—are far more likely to remain in their positions when they feel supported by administrators, have strong bonds of connection to colleagues, and are aggressively pursuing a collective vision for student learning about which they feel passion and commitment. Teachers' connections to the profession and to their schools are also strengthened when they feel they possess

the content knowledge, instructional skills, and technological tools to meet the challenges of standards-based education in increasingly diverse classrooms. (Sparks, 2002, p. 4)

The recommendations of the National Commission on Teaching and America's Future (NCTAF) are consistent with those of NSDC. In its report *No Dream Denied: A Pledge to America's Children*, NCTAF (2003) notes that the era of solo teaching in isolated classrooms is over:

Good teaching thrives in a supportive learning environment created by teachers and school leaders who work together to improve learning—in short, quality teaching requires strong, professional learning communities. Collegial interchange, not isolation, must become the norm for teachers. (p. 17)

The Importance of Leaving Nothing to Chance

The evidence is clear: school leaders cannot leave new teacher development to chance. Leaders must be proactive and put time and resources behind the support and development of Tweeners. By doing this, we can methodically create the positive school cultures we need for our schools to universally evolve into high-performing organizations. Our schools' future is in jeopardy if we cannot create a system that protects and grooms our Tweeners into the type of educators that will achieve longevity in the field and adopt the types of philosophies and practices that increase student learning. Paying close attention to their needs and developing systems of support will go a long way in reducing the turnover rate. Socializing them in the progressive and visionary goals of public school will ensure that Tweeners do more than stay in the profession; it will ensure their effectiveness for years to come.

CHAPTER 5

The Survivors

During the course of this study, a small but important group of teachers emerged. This group was not large in number, and in most cases, leaders responded appropriately to their needs. I call this group the Survivors. A Survivor is an educator who has completely given up on practicing effective instruction and has focused his or her energy on a new mission: survival until the end of the school year—and in some cases, the end of the school day. The Survivors made up less than 2 percent of the educators observed in this study, but if gone unchecked, they can have an absolutely devastating impact on their students' chances of receiving a quality education.

A comprehensive study conducted at the University of Tennessee shows that students assigned to ineffective teachers continue to show the effects of such teachers even when those students are subsequently assigned to very effective teachers (Sanders & Rivers, 1996). The residual effects of both very effective and ineffective teachers are measurable two years later, regardless of the teachers' effectiveness in later grades. The same study also finds that students who have three effective teachers or three ineffective teachers in a row have vastly different achievement levels. Because of differences in teacher effectiveness, students whose achievement levels were similar in mathematics at the beginning of third grade scored 50 percentile points apart on fifth-grade achievement tests just three years later. Poor and ineffective instruction can completely undermine the school's fundamental mission. This is why leaders must remove teachers who have become burnt-out or depressed from the classroom and address their issues. It is what is best for the student as well as the teacher.

In this chapter, I'll discuss the Survivors in regard to:

- Flight response
- Student bargaining
- Pedagogical characteristics
- Organizational response
- Stress and pressure

Flight Response

When human beings face stress that becomes overwhelming, they psychologically retreat to a safer place, away from the overwhelming stress. The field of education is very demanding, and practitioners face many challenges both in and outside of the classroom. These challenges include classroom organization, lesson planning, student evaluation, discipline, parent and community relations, and administrative requirements. All of these responsibilities can cause some moments of extreme stress for even the most prepared and experienced educators.

However, there's a distinction between workplace stress and what has been categorized as *burnout*. According to *Preventing Burnout: Signs, Symptoms, and Strategies to Avoid It*, "Workplace burnout isn't the same as workplace stress. When you're stressed, you care too much, but when you're burned out, you don't see any hope of improvement" (Smith, Jaffe-Gill, Segal, & Segal, 2007, p. 2). Nearly everyone experiences workplace stress, but people who have burnout have become shells of their former selves; the psychological flight response has been triggered, and they descend into depression.

Teri McCarthy-Wood and Chris Wood (2002) trace the development of teacher burnout:

> When a potentially threatening event is encountered, a reflexive, cognitive balancing act ensues, weighing the perceived demands of the event against one's perceived ability to deal with them. Events perceived as potential threats trigger the

stress response, a series of physiological and psychological changes that occur when coping capacities are seriously
challenged. The most typical trigger to the stress response
is the perception that ones' coping resources are inadequate for handling life demands. . . . Teacher stress may be
seen as the perception of an imbalance between demands
at school and the resources teachers have for coping with
them. Symptoms of stress in teachers can include anxiety
and frustration, impaired performance, and ruptured interper-
sonal relationships at work and home. (pp. 109–110)

A 2016 report on the state of the teaching profession reveals that one
out of every five new teachers entering the classroom in urban schools is
grossly unprepared (Sutcher, Darling-Hammond, & Carver-Thomas,
2016). Placing unprepared teachers in an environment where students
come to school with high academic and emotional needs is a recipe for
disaster. Yvette Jackson refers to our neediest students as *school dependent* instead of *at risk*; because if they do not receive certain academic
and moral direction at school, the likelihood of them ever receiving
that guidance outside of school is highly unlikely (Jackson, 2011). This
dilemma requires that schools with school-dependent students hire the
most prepared teachers to address the most dependent students' needs.
Unfortunately this is not the case; grossly underprepared teachers, coupled with high-needs students, creates the conditions that lead to the
systemic creation of Survivors.

GERM's (NCLB and ESSA) impact has been even more detrimental
to educators who would struggle, even under the best circumstances.
A 2012 Vanderbilt University study that analyzes NCLB's effect on
teachers' perception and morale concludes that NCLB produced some
very tangible negative effects on teachers, including a significantly negative impact of four different job satisfiers (Grissom, Nicholson-Crotty,
& Harrington, 2014): (1) job satisfaction, (2) intent to remain in the
profession, (3) wage satisfaction, and (4) work hours. NCLB and ESSA
demand more of teachers personally and professionally in an environment of high stress, declining resources, and flat or decreasing compen-
sation. These factors have an even greater impact on our professionals
with significant professional skill gaps.

The balancing act that teachers have to perform is very real. Unfortunately, the consequences of an inability to handle this balancing act of student, parent, colleague, and administration demands can adversely affect both a person's psychological and physical well-being. Survivors should not be ridiculed or demeaned; their condition is real, and they require help.

Student Bargaining

What became immediately apparent to me in this study was that the Survivors were not in control of their own emotions, which made it difficult for them to manage others' behavior, particularly students. Students are adept at quickly identifying the teachers who have reached this level of withdrawal, and they take advantage of the situation.

With life at work spiraling out of control, it is surprising that Survivors can actually manage to make it from day to day and year to year. They do so by engaging in tacit, informal bargaining with their students. The Survivor extends an olive branch to students and offers them the opportunity to bargain for the conditions that would allow for a peaceful coexistence. In a nutshell, Survivors want to know what it will take for students to agree to leave them alone.

Students, of course, seize this opportunity to gain privileges that they know would never be allowed in other classes. I witnessed some of the spoils of their shrewd bargaining.

- Use of banned electronic items such as music devices and video games

- Access to the computer for personal purposes

- Access to nonacademic television and video programs

- Opportunities to bring food and beverages into the classroom

- Receipt of favorable grades in exchange for compliance with the teacher

As long as students are happy and compliant, this system remains intact. The students get what they want, and the teacher gets what he or she wants. As long as this agreement is in place, the class appears to an unsuspecting supervisor as orderly and harmonious. But this system tends to break down on a regular basis. Some students become increasingly demanding, and those concerned with achievement become frustrated with the lack of learning opportunities and begin to involve their parents. When this happened during my study, the administration was forced to act. We will examine its response in the latter part of this chapter.

Pedagogical Characteristics

Survivors' psychological withdrawal causes many observable characteristics. The Survivors carry no political agenda. Their sole purpose is to make it to the end of each school day with their sanity intact. They do not interact much with other educators, and when they do, the conversation is usually of a personal nature. *Shop talk* is not something Survivors value or engage in.

The absence of good professional practice is a Survivor's most noticeable and damaging characteristic. In fact, many of the Survivors I observed showed no evidence of professional practice or even the desire to use good professional practices. I regularly observed the following teaching techniques from Survivors.

- Frequent use of video as a primary teaching tool

- Frequent use of the computer lab for nonacademic reasons

- Frequent use of worksheets as busywork to fill time

- Frequent granting of free time as a reward for behavioral cooperation

The Survivors I observed were not very well-respected among their peers. All the stakeholders in the organization agreed that the Survivors were not good for the school and condemned their practices universally. Many educators felt sympathy for them, but there was consensus that Survivors did not belong in the classroom in their current state of mind.

Organizational Response

When professionals, especially those responsible for students' well-being, reach a point where they spiral into a pit of depression that they cannot dig themselves out of, the organization must respond and respond swiftly. The organization cannot ignore or easily fix the Survivor's state. The best and only real solution is to remove the Survivor from the conditions that caused the depression until he or she can get proper treatment (Haberman, 2005). Wishful thinking or turning a blind eye will not solve the problem, and leaving Survivors in the environment that caused their psychological breakdown can only make matters worse.

In the cases I observed, the administration generally used the following methods to deal with Survivors.

- Reassigned the teacher to a less challenging teaching assignment

- Worked with officials to have the teacher transferred to another school within the district with the hope that a change in environment might be invigorating

- Counseled the teacher into retirement, if that option was available

- Ignored the symptoms and responded harshly to the disruptive students in an attempt to force them to cooperate with the teacher

- Dealt strictly with the professional behavior without considering the cause and responded harshly to the teacher through a series of punitive measures for nonperformance

- Sought the teacher's removal through termination or some form of medical leave

Stress and Pressure

The stress that comes with working in schools is very real. Pressure from all sides—administration, colleagues, students and their families, the community at large, the government, and a teacher's responsibilities at home—can cause anyone to have a bad day from time to time. But when these pressures become overwhelming, they can do real physical and psychological damage. When teachers burn out and succumb to the daily stress, neither they nor their students benefit. They become locked in a nonproductive, educationally stagnant environment, and swift action and intervention by those in authority are necessary.

The good news is that many school leaders do act to reduce the effects Survivors have on students. All the administrators I observed in my study acted—they did not turn their heads and pretend that the problem did not exist. In all but one case, the Survivor was removed from the situation, and as a result the classroom conditions drastically and instantly improved. In several cases, the district provided psychological treatment and paid employment leave through its insurance carrier, and the educators had an opportunity to return if the treating physician cleared them. When these conditions manifest, the best we can hope to do is to shield the educator and the students from further damage.

CHAPTER 6

The Fundamentalists

Of the four types of educators I observed in schools and classrooms during my study, the two with the most influence and importance to school culture are the Believers and the Fundamentalists. A Fundamentalist is an experienced educator who believes that there is one pure and undisputable way to practice: the traditional model of schooling. Fundamentalists are the vanguards of tradition and protect the status quo. They are relentless in their attempts to discourage change and protect a system that has allowed them to function and thrive, and they organize to protect this traditional way of practice. Their experiences have led them to believe that the traditional model of schooling is the best and purest model. It is the system that was used to educate them, and it is the system they were socialized into when they became new professionals. They have learned that system's rules, and they understand how it functions and how to excel within it. They view change itself as an enemy; therefore, anyone who challenges the system is a threat to the system and a threat to the Fundamentalists. They are the most aggressive and vocal combatants in this war of ideology.

The dictionary defines *fundamentalism* as "a movement or attitude stressing strict and literal adherence to a set of basic principles," and a *fundamentalist* as one that strongly adheres to a basic set of beliefs even when facing criticism or unpopularity ("fundamentalism," 2017). Even though the term *fundamentalist* is often used in the religious arena, it clearly applies to people and belief systems outside of religion.

Any school leader interested in producing a healthy school culture must understand the Fundamentalists and how they operate. They pose the biggest threat to change and improvement in our school system. Albert Einstein is quoted as saying that insanity is defined as "doing the same thing over and over again and expecting a different result" (as cited in Tangredi, 2005). If our schools are going to improve student learning, they must embrace strategies that are radically different from those we have embraced in the past. An organization that does not evolve does not improve. An organization that does not improve is doomed to fail. Fundamentalists do not intend to destroy or ruin schools. Quite the contrary: they believe their paradigm is correct, that standing up for what they believe in is pure and fundamental, and that they will indeed save the institution. But their stance causes a dilemma. Leaders are being pushed to make meaningful and substantive change in schools, which means that some practices and values will have to change. This immediately puts leaders at odds with Fundamentalists, who are zealous about maintaining the status quo and tradition.

In this chapter, I'll discuss Fundamentalists in regard to the following characteristics and explain why a necessary evolution is in order.

- Opposition to change
- The Old Contract versus the New Contract
- Belief in the normal distribution
- Skill levels
- Warring paradigms
- The three Ds (*defamation*, *disruption*, and *distraction*)

Opposition to Change

The Fundamentalist's most distinctive characteristic is a blatant and overt opposition to change. Indeed, change disrupts the organization's natural flow and represents a realignment of values. It is important to note that Fundamentalists enjoy practicing as professional educators. They enjoy the traditional aspects of the school as an institution. While observing and interviewing Fundamentalists, I saw a clear affinity for this tradition: Fundamentalists often speak fondly of the days when corporal punishment, curricular autonomy, and local control were part and parcel of our education system. They express a loathing for outside influence and control and administrators who dare to try to control operations in their classrooms. Where does this tendency to cling to the past come from?

Dan Lortie's (2002) sociological study reveals some critical information about teachers. Lortie (2002) observes two very important variables that may explain the behavior of Fundamentalists.

1. Teachers have been socialized in the education field since kindergarten, having spent thousands of hours as students. Since age five, educators observed others' practice in the field in which they would eventually practice themselves. Lortie (2002) calls this phenomenon the *apprenticeship of observation*.

2. On average, teachers were very good students and occupied the highest levels of the organization. As teachers, they bring that experience to the classroom and seek to preserve the same system that they enjoyed and benefited from as students.

Lortie (2002) concludes that it is irrational to expect people who benefited from a system to be the catalyst for changing that system. In fact, we should expect them to try to preserve a personally beneficial system. This helps explain why Fundamentalists would have such reverence for traditional school norms and values and why they would feel threatened if those traditional ideas were challenged or eventually replaced. The educator's own personal experience in school, according to Lortie, is the single most important variable in the current paradigm of the schoolteacher.

Lortie's (2002) research is helpful in clarifying many values that Fundamentalists hold dear; Fundamentalists collectively long for the way that schools used to operate. This longing can be described in what I call the *Old Contract* and the *New Contract*.

The Old Contract Versus the New Contract

The Old Contract represents the unwritten set of norms, values, and practices that defined the public school system for both students and educators before the advent of the accountability movement. The New Contract is the new set of values that promote transparency of school performance to the public, standardized curriculum and assessments, and proficiency ratings that nonmembers of the school community determined, along with the new educational strategies that support that system. In this case, the term *contract* refers to the universal set of expectations that guides every member of the school community and defines his or her roles and responsibilities within the context of the public school system. In many cases, Fundamentalists entered the field while these long-held traditions were still in place, and they expressed discontent and anguish over the new paradigms and systems that have replaced them, which has further solidified their opposition to change in general.

The Old Contract provision that seems to find the most Fundamentalist approval is a teacher's right to autonomy. The most oft-repeated credo I heard from Fundamentalists was the teacher's right to control curriculum. From the very beginning of the evolution of American schools, teachers had the right to control what content they taught in their classroom. The Old Contract dictated that the system had the right to choose the general theme and focus for the class through some form of master course schedule (mathematics, reading, algebra 1, and so on), but the specific content to be covered during instruction was the individual classroom teacher's exclusive right. The teacher determined the content of the lesson, how it was taught, and the pace of instruction.

The New Contract calls for a standardized curriculum. A central body, usually a state department of education, developed this curriculum, and teachers are expected to teach students defined learning standards. Fundamentalists collectively display a dislike for "outsiders" such as administrators, boards of education, and politicians interfering with what many call their "creativity." A common complaint among those I observed was that they do not have enough time to be creative and teach what they want to teach to students because they have lost control of the curriculum. Fundamentalists are convinced that the standardized curriculum is detrimental to students, and they express this viewpoint to anyone willing to listen. They yearn to go back to the

Exclusive Videos from
Anthony Muhammad, Richard DuFour, Tim Brown, and Luis Cruz

Get dynamic supplemental content for the newest edition of this best-selling book while gaining immediate, accessible strategies you can use the very next day to build a healthy school environment.

CHAPTER 1: *From Status Quo to True Reform*

Social Response to Inequality
– *Anthony Muhammad*
  ▶ *8:16*

CHAPTER 2: *The Framework of Modern School Culture*

Changing the Culture of an Organization
– *Anthony Muhammad*
  ▶ *7:04*

The Culture of an Effective PLC School
– *Richard DuFour*
  ▶ *6:36*

Other videos available online

CHAPTER 3: *The Believers*

Transforming School Culture: The Believers
– *Anthony Muhammad*
  ▶ *7:09*

Creating a Data Picture of Your School with Your Leadership Team – *Anthony Muhammad*
  ▶ *7:53*

Other videos available online

CHAPTER 4: *The Tweeners*

Transforming School Culture: The Tweeners
– *Anthony Muhammad*
  ▶ *10:13*

CLAIM YOUR FREE TRIAL
SolutionTree.com/GlobalPD

Solution Tree

Old Contract, according to which teachers had the right to shut their doors and teach students the things they felt were most important to learn. Losing the right to curricular autonomy has been particularly painful for Fundamentalists.

Fundamentalists also express displeasure with losing autonomy over evaluation. Under the Old Contract, teachers not only had the right to teach the things they felt students should learn but also were afforded the right to be the sole assessors of student proficiency. Under the Old Contract, teacher judgment was the sole criterion for determining student academic success. Under the New Contract, proficiency is judged both internally and externally by student performance on standardized academic exams. Additionally, the New Contract has created an atmosphere that places blame on the teacher for failing to prepare students properly for success, whereas the Old Contract placed the blame on the student for not reaching proficiency. This represents a substantial shift in practice and philosophy.

The Old Contract recognized the teacher as not only the content expert but also the instructional expert. The Old Contract assumed that teachers were not only knowledgeable about the subject they taught, by virtue of going through the rites of passage necessary to attain a professional teaching position, but also experts on how to teach that content. This assumption created space between the teacher and outside influences; teachers were the undisputed masters of their roles. The New Contract does not make such a defined distinction. The era of accountability has caused educators in leadership positions to become involved in instruction and instructional development in new ways. Stakes are high for school districts; if students do not excel on standardized tests, government officials want to know what school or district leaders plan to do to improve student performance. This new role of instructional leadership has particularly annoyed Fundamentalists. In my study, many Fundamentalists expressed displeasure with leadership activities such as administrative walkthroughs, common academic assessments, student achievement data, and other intrusions on instructional autonomy. They also resented the new push to constantly seek professional development and to use terms like *research based* and *best practice*. To Fundamentalists, these concepts and terms are an insult to their expertise and intelligence. They feel that the New Contract interferes with their ability to be as effective as they once were in their classrooms.

The Old Contract gave teachers freedom of interaction. If teachers chose to shut the door and avoid interaction with colleagues, they were free to do so. If their classroom was orderly, students behaved, and they attempted to teach their subject matter, teachers had the right to be left alone. In fact, when I started as a teacher in 1988 in Lansing, Michigan, my school culture taught me that I would be well-respected among my peers if I could demonstrate that I could operate effectively without the help of others. So, under the Old Contract, not only did teachers have a right to work in isolation, they were *rewarded* for taking a position of isolation.

Under the New Contract, schools are demanding that teachers work together and collaborate as a new strategy to help student academic performance. Not only does the concept annoy Fundamentalists, but the terminology does as well. Fundamentalists do not feel the need to work with others. They feel that they have paid the price to enter the field and that they know enough to teach their students properly without attending collaborative meetings at the building or district levels. The overwhelming majority of Fundamentalists I studied felt that meeting with other teachers was a waste of time and an intrusion of their right to control their working conditions. Having their day dictated and planned for them was not a part of the initial deal.

Finally, Fundamentalists resent the new role of students, parents, and the community at large. Under the Old Contract, students were admonished to obey and listen to their teachers or punitive measures would swiftly follow. At one juncture, teachers could physically punish students who did not comply. Under the Old Contract, it was the school leaders' job to support the teacher by either removing or punishing any student who did not comply with directives or posed a threat to classroom harmony. Fundamentalists were very comfortable with the principal's role under those circumstances. The Old Contract also dictated that parents had limited access and influence in the classroom. The teacher, and the school in general, prevailed in issues of grades, behavior, and privileges. The business of the school belonged to those who were the experts and professionals.

The New Contract looks very different. Litigious parents and a society with a thirst for negative media coverage have redefined how schools interact with the community. Administrators have to consider school, district, and legal policies before disciplining a student. In fact, under No Child Left Behind, if a school fails to meet stated academic progress goals, parents have the right to enroll their child in another school at the school system's cost (for transportation and so on). Fundamentalists feel that the New Contract has produced an anti-teacher climate in our schools.

It is very evident that Fundamentalists do not have much confidence or admiration for the current direction of public education. Fundamentalists do not view themselves as anti-education or anti-student, they simply hold a different set of beliefs than those of the new era of public education. They feel that the Old Contract has a proven track record and is more fair and equitable than the New Contract.

Belief in the Normal Distribution

In chapter 1, we examined the phenomenon of the bell curve and normal distributions and established that in a normal distribution, equity is not the goal; rather, comparison and ranking are the goals. Herrnstein and Murray (1994) argue in *The Bell Curve* that this is simply the natural order of things, that all things are not equal and will never be equal; some human beings happen to be more talented, gifted, and capable than others, and anyone who does not acknowledge this reality is delusional. Fundamentalists hold a very similar paradigm.

As I interviewed Fundamentalist educators, I learned that they loathed accountability initiatives like NCLB, and they did not agree with the mantra that "all students can learn." One Fundamentalist told me:

> It is impossible for every kid to excel in school. Some of them are cut out for school, and some just are not. I listen to the principal giving "lip service" about believing in all kids, but he knows as well as I do that that just isn't going to happen.

This statement was typical of a Fundamentalist response to the egalitarian ideal that schools can be places where equity in learning is possible.

Even more interesting, each Fundamentalist with whom I had an opportunity to interact did not feel that his or her stance was pessimistic or anti-student. Fundamentalists felt their viewpoint was simply more realistic—that anyone who believed every student in the United States could read and perform mathematics at grade level by the year 2013 was either not rooted in reality or under the influence of a controlled substance! The goal of NCLB was not realized. The year 2013 has come and gone, and we still have not reached the goal of universal mathematics and reading proficiency among all American students. In the Fundamentalist's mind, educators and politicians who promote universal achievement for students need a paradigm shift. In fact, some Fundamentalists expressed that they believed egalitarian idealism is in fact damaging for students who face tremendous obstacles to school performance like poverty and unfit parents. One Fundamentalist expressed concern that these students felt they were "set up for disappointment." She elaborated by saying, "These kids do not need to be fooled into believing they can all go to college when many of them were born crack-cocaine dependent or suffered from fetal alcohol syndrome." She felt that they would be better off if they instead had more access to trades or classes where they could "use their hands." Another Fundamentalist supported this worldview with a simple statement, "We live in a world where some people are doctors, and some people pick up garbage." He and others felt that this societal polarization was the natural order of things, and who was he to mess with nature? It would be fair for Fundamentalists to see NCLB as governmental overreach, but not validation for a *social Darwinist* attitude. John Hattie (2012) proves that the teacher's prediction of student success has the greatest impact on student achievement. The evidence is clear that their pessimistic attitudes and low expectations are much more damaging than NCLB or ESSA.

Fundamentalists can be accurately described as *social Darwinists*. Sociologist Robert Bannister (2010) describes social Darwinism as:

The idea that humans, like animals and plants, compete in a struggle for existence in which natural selection results in "survival of the fittest." Social Darwinists typically deny that they advocate a "law of the jungle." But most propose arguments that justify imbalances of power between individuals, races, and nations because they consider some people more fit to survive than others. (p. 1)

Social stratification is a norm to Fundamentalists. They believe that some people, for some reason, are simply more capable than others, and this natural and eternal imbalance is a function of the universe.

Upon examination of Fundamentalists' classroom performance, I discovered that their paradigm was philosophical, and they also translated this belief system into practice. Their student grade distribution generally held to the standard of a normal distribution of performance. They assigned a small percentage of As, and the vast majority of students received Bs, Cs, and Ds, and usually a small proportion of students received Fs. This was true except in classes that were made up of large numbers of students labeled *at risk* or *honors*. In these cases, the grade distributions were skewed to either pole depending on the class makeup.

The Fundamentalists also shared similar discipline patterns. They did not write excessive amounts of referrals; they simply referred students for discipline who fit the typical profile of students in need of control through punitive methods. These students included a disproportionate amount of minority students and male students who did not excel at the secondary level. At the elementary level, they disproportionately referred students who did not display grade-appropriate maturity. In many cases, they also encouraged administrators to test students for placement in special education.

There was a clear disconnect between student performance and teacher responsibility among the Fundamentalists I observed. Fundamentalists clearly believed that students should sink or swim on their own merits. Those who excel deserve the fruits of their labor, they suggested, and those who do not excel deserve their fate because of a lack of personal commitment or ability. They expressed little to no empathy for students who were not successful, and they also did not try to take credit for the students who excelled. Their job was to allow nature to take its course.

Skill Levels

Like Believers, Fundamentalists display a wide range of professional skill. I observed some Fundamentalists who displayed very low levels of content knowledge and pedagogical skills and others who displayed high levels of knowledge and used very effective teaching strategies with their students.

A Fundamentalist is not an ineffective teacher by virtue of his or her political stance. But certain values Fundamentalists hold dear make it very difficult for them to promote a healthy school culture. Fundamentalists who I observed using very effective teaching strategies were effective with the students that they were entrusted to educate, but they still refused to work well with other professionals or embrace any form of change, and they had a generally negative disposition about their leaders' motives and ability.

I contend that even the most effective Fundamentalists still pose a threat to a school's culture and its achievement of universal success for all students. Even though they show pockets of effectiveness and proficiency, they are not poised to embrace techniques and strategies that could allow them to be even more effective. Obviously, a Fundamentalist who does *not* exhibit effectiveness in the classroom is an even bigger problem. An ineffective professional who rejects change presents a danger to any organization.

Warring Paradigms

Of all members of the school community, Fundamentalists are by far the most active. They actively and consistently seek to add to their ranks and to gain political power to support their belief system. They are very active within the formal and informal organization, and their level of commitment to achieving their end is much more intense than that of the Believers. Watching them operate within several different school systems revealed a savvy, well-organized, and determined group of individuals. I found that they tended to be more emotional rather than rational, and formal rather than informal.

Emotional Versus Rational

Fundamentalists kept the philosophical argument focused on emotion. They regularly engaged in debates, sometimes arguments, with staff members with opposing viewpoints. During these debates, they centered their arguments about how a proposed policy change or change in practice affected them and other staff members on the emotional issues associated with the change—on comfort, convenience, and working conditions.

At an elementary school, I observed a school-improvement team meeting at which the Fundamentalists quickly took control. The meeting consisted of seven staff members from the school: five teachers, one school psychologist, and the principal. The team discussed a proposed change in the recess schedule: under the new plan, students would receive a recess of twenty minutes daily, which was in compliance with state law and met the teacher contractual time allotment, instead of the thirty minutes they currently received. Lunchroom aides traditionally supervised recess at this school, and that would continue under the principal's proposed plan. Teachers typically used the thirty minutes per day to plan lessons, correct papers, or for other school-related work. The principal explained that the extra ten minutes per day would be used to extend a literacy block for students and that this extra time was critical for struggling readers, especially in grades 3 through 5.

Her proposal met immediate resistance by two of the seven members, who were Fundamentalists. The first teacher spoke as if she had gathered a coalition of teachers who felt that they currently had too much responsibility, and taking ten minutes from the thirty minutes of undirected teacher time would cause immediate resistance within the ranks of teachers. The second teacher expressed concern about infringements on her "personal time." She expressed concern about losing control of noninstructional time, and suggested that giving in to this proposal might be the beginning of a domino effect that could develop into a total loss of control of professional time, both instructional and noninstructional.

The principal appeared to be unprepared for their responses. She immediately tried to meet them at an emotional level by questioning their commitment to the school's fundamental purpose. She expressed concern about what she considered "professionals squabbling over a mere ten minutes per day." The principal missed the point. Her anger over the two Fundamentalists' answers created a psychological impasse that caused both parties to retreat to their corners, and the issue remained unresolved. The other team members sat silently at a distance as the Fundamentalists went to battle with the school principal.

What lay at the heart of the position of the two Fundamentalists?

- Personal comfort

- Attachment to their daily routine

- Resistance to giving up power

The principal fell right into the emotional argument of the Fundamentalists, and they achieved exactly what they intended: *protection of the status quo.* Fundamentalists thrive at the emotional level. They rarely challenge an organizational change that research and empirical evidence support concerning the purpose of schooling and effective education of students. What is even more fascinating is that Believers, both teachers and administrators, rarely challenge Fundamentalists with research-supported arguments.

The principal in the meeting I observed was offering changes that would support the organization's stated goals. She wanted to improve her students' literacy skills, especially at the upper-elementary level where students performed more than 20 percent below the state average on her state's standardized reading test at grades 3, 4, and 5. She could have buttressed her case with research supporting longer exposure to effective literacy strategies to promote student proficiency in reading. Instead, she allowed the Fundamentalists to engage her in an emotional argument, the catalyst for yet another Fundamentalist victory in her school. Things remained the same, despite the fact that large numbers of students did not achieve at acceptable levels academically.

If Believers are to effect change, they must engage Fundamentalists in discussion. Believers should remember that engaging a Fundamentalist in an emotional battle is not a recipe for success. Believers must instead use the following three-step approach.

1. Clearly state the reason for the change proposal.

2. Connect the change proposal to the school's foundational purpose and the stated improvement goals with the use of objective information (data).

3. Support the proposal with empirical and anecdotal evidence of effectiveness from several different sources.

This three-step approach erodes the Fundamentalists' argument at the foundation. It reasserts the fact that schools are built for the education of children. It puts students at the center of the argument, and it makes it difficult for Fundamentalists to publicly advocate for a stance that clearly hurts children. Finally, this type of approach forces Fundamentalists to present an equally compelling argument that empirical evidence supports. When Believers used these strategies in the schools I observed, the Fundamentalists' political power took a major hit, especially in formal organizational settings.

Formal Versus Informal Culture

Organizational theorists agree that every organization has both a formal and informal structure. Henry Landsberger first introduced this concept in the famous study of the Hawthorne Works plant in Cicero, Illinois, from 1924–1932. The conclusions from this study sparked a series of important findings in workplace relations and employee productivity (Pyöriä, 2007).

The *formal organization* consists of all the organization's official arms. The organizational structure has officially sanctioned these branches of the organization. These branches consist of official committees, task forces, and teams such as school-improvement teams, curriculum committees, and the parent-teacher association (PTA). Parts of the formal organization are monitored and evaluated against the organization's norms and goals.

The *informal organization* consists of all covert alliances that develop as a result of interaction in the formal organization. These alliances are not officially sanctioned, and their members create their goals, so they are only governed by those who participate. They have no formal rules. An informal alliance's goals are generally not in alignment with those of the formal organization, which often makes the informal organization a threat to the formal organization's productivity and longevity (Pyöriä, 2007). Fundamentalists work very effectively in the informal organization.

It became very clear after spending hours observing and interviewing Tweeners that they were prime targets of Fundamentalist recruitment in the informal organization. These informal situations tended to form in staff lounges, staff parking lots, during telephone or email conversations, at official and unofficial staff social events, and in the school halls. These informal places allowed the Fundamentalist to bond with other Fundamentalists and potential Fundamentalists. In these informal arenas, Fundamentalists can control the agenda and form the argument. Believers are intentionally omitted from informal Fundamentalist alliances unless they are viewed as potential converts.

Unless a school leader concerned about improving the quality of student learning is skilled in organizational politics, these informal alliances could easily go undetected and work against progress. A school leader must always be aware of the conversations happening around him or her, both formal and informal, and develop the skill of "erasing the line" between the informal and formal organizations. Staff members must become as comfortable expressing their views in the public forum, under the norms and values of the formal organization, as they are expressing them in the informal organization's privacy. In order to accomplish this end, leaders must accomplish the following two objectives.

1. **Create frequent opportunities for Fundamentalists to voice their viewpoint**, and be prepared to refute potential arguments against change initiatives by stating a better and more profound public case.

2. **Extend a public olive branch to opposing viewpoints by encouraging intellectual dialogue about organizational goals**. This objective will help others see that leaders are not seeking to perpetuate division among staff members, and they may come to view Fundamentalists' informal recruitment as unethical.

The Three Ds

The pattern of the Fundamentalist is very predictable. I observed Fundamentalists using three primary methods of influence to achieve their political ends: (1) defamation, (2) disruption, and (3) distraction. These methods were sequential, and the intensity of their potency declined with the use of each method.

Defamation

Within the most stagnant and toxic of school cultures, Fundamentalists rule by intimidation. They are not shy about letting visitors know that they control the direction of the organization. At this very toxic stage, leaders must be extremely careful about the approach they take when initially challenging the Fundamentalists' control of the organization. The first method I observed Fundamentalists using when threatened was defamation—an all-out personal assault on the change agent. When someone challenges a toxic culture, Fundamentalists most often attack the individual advocating the change.

In my study, I witnessed this form of assault at a middle school situated in a suburban school district near a major midwestern city. The district used to be very racially homogeneous (white) and middle class. Then, the district experienced a huge transformation of demographics both racially and economically. In 2006, the school district was 91 percent African American, and 40 percent of the students in the district were from homes that were economically disadvantaged.

The district was experiencing all the typical transition issues associated with this type of massive cultural and economic change in the community. Educational consultant and author Jawanza Kunjufu (2002) identifies these struggles in the following manner.

- There is a cultural disconnection between the experienced staff and the new student population.

- School employees, particularly teachers and administrators, do not reflect the student body racially, culturally, and economically.

- There is a policy and systemic disconnection between the
  school system and the new community members.

The district hired its first African American superintendent in 2002,
and one of her initial goals was to hire a more diverse staff with an emphasis on district and building leadership. This initiative did not bode well
with the teacher and administrator union leaders, who claimed that past
practice dictated that the district should promote experienced teachers
with long-term histories and commitments to the district to key leadership positions. The unions felt that intentionally seeking candidates on
the basis of race would damage that long-standing tradition of awarding
leadership positions to those who knew the district best.

The superintendent did not agree with the union's assertion. She felt
that leadership positions had been traditionally given to experienced
teachers who were politically connected and who wished to pad their
retirement packages by spending the final years of their educational
careers as administrators who enjoyed higher salaries. The superintendent presented the board of education and the union with data from
the past twenty years illustrating that the typical building principal was
in the twilight of his or her career and stayed in the position an average of 3.2 years. She argued that not only did the district need more
diverse representation in the ranks of leadership, but that the good ol'
boy system of politically motivated leadership assignments needed to
be changed as well.

The middle school hired an African American woman to serve as
principal in 2005. She was not only the first African American principal, but also the first woman to serve in that position. Additionally, she
was the first external hire for this leadership position in the previous
eighteen years. She had over twenty-five years of experience as a teacher
and administrator in a large urban school district. The superintendent
appointed her to the position based on her impressive interview with
the superintendent and her cabinet. The building teaching staff were
not involved in the interview process for the new principal, despite the
fact that teachers had been involved in that process for over thirty years.
It was well-known that many staff members wanted to see the current
assistant principal, a former teacher, promoted to the top position.

The Fundamentalists were upset with these new developments for two reasons.

1. The traditional system of promotion to leadership was dismantled. This new reality might affect some Fundamentalists directly and affect their future plans and incomes.

2. The new superintendent disregarded the traditional power structure. The unions had been powerful forces in demanding the conditions for selecting personnel. If the unions lost political power, Fundamentalists' input and power as district employees were in jeopardy.

The new principal represented this great shift in control of power. Though the vast majority of the experienced teachers who embraced the traditional district system and policies were white, some were African American. In fact, about one-third of the staff was African American. Their issue with the new principal was motivated by power: they sought to maintain a system that they felt was more personally beneficial.

The Fundamentalist defamation campaign against the new principal had two facets. The first case they tried to make was that her experience in an urban district was not compatible with what they needed in their suburban district. Many of the Fundamentalists referred to her as the "ghetto principal" in private. The second case they tried to establish centered on her student disciplinary philosophy. The new principal wrote a memo to the staff in the first month of her tenure in response to what she considered to be a high number of disciplinary referrals for students. She believed that a student should only be suspended from school under the most extreme circumstances. The Fundamentalists ran with this philosophy and tried to make the case that student conduct was out of control and the school was going in the wrong direction.

The Fundamentalists were very active in the informal organization, making the case to both staff members and parents that the principal's urban experience was subpar, and she was unprepared to lead a traditionally high-achieving school. Fundamentalists openly discussed what they considered her lack of qualifications with anyone who would listen. The defamation campaign about the student suspension issue was prosecuted in the several different arenas. This issue made its way into the gossip circles, but there were also two formal employee grievances filed on behalf of staff members who felt that her leadership made the building "unsafe" for students and teachers—even though the facts revealed that under her tenure, serious student violations like assaults, drug use, weapon possession, and theft were down significantly from the previous school year.

This two-pronged approach caused such uproar within the school and community that the board put pressure on the superintendent to reassign the principal after just two years of service at the middle school. The union leaders used the ousted principal's "failure" as a rationale to reinstitute the old site-based interview process that they claimed was more effective. The superintendent did not want to honor this request.

The new principal represented a threat to everything that the Fundamentalists had come to know. They believed that if they allowed this administrative appointment to go unchallenged, nothing would be off limits. The need for power and control motivated their actions, and defaming and undermining the new principal were just collateral damage.

This aggressive campaign of defamation is not unfamiliar to our culture. Modern political campaigns are rooted in the notion that if we publicly destroy and humiliate our opponent, we increase our chances of success (Ordway & Wihbey, 2017). Our culture seems to have a fascination with scandal, and being caught in a scandal is extremely damaging. Fundamentalists choose defamation as a tool of organizational control because it is so effective.

Disruption

When defamation is not enough, Fundamentalists turn to disruption and delay the implementation of policies or strategies that will force them to change their practices. So if the messenger cannot be stopped, the change initiative itself becomes the target.

On several occasions, I observed Fundamentalists engaged in creating what I call *miscellaneous scenarios*: obstacles to implementing change that are so overwhelming that the staff loses confidence in the proposed change. For example, an interdisciplinary middle school team met about a proposed change to its student homework policy. A team member I had identified as a Believer initiated the proposal. The rationale for the policy change was data the district academic office gave to the team; these data showed that during the first semester of the school year, 40 percent of their students had either a D or an F on their report cards. This number was much higher than the district average of just over 20 percent. The policy change proposed the following provisions.

- Students would be allowed to turn in assignments after the due date, with a penalty to be determined by the team.

- Students would have an amnesty period of two days during which they could voluntarily enter a homework-assistance hour to be held after school. Teachers would volunteer their time and rotate the duty of supervising this homework-assistance hour.

- Teachers would send a letter to students' homes to notify parents when students were missing two assignments, and teachers would make a personal phone call when students had more than four missing assignments.

These proposals triggered a barrage of "What if?" scenarios from the vocal Fundamentalist on the team. She immediately attacked the logistical aspects of the proposal but not the proposal's philosophical or theoretical aspects. Before considering the provisions of the proposal, she made the following rebuttals.

- "What if students wait until the last possible moment to turn in their assignments, and we get stuck grading a lot of papers?"

- "Who is going to decide the varying degrees of *late*? Will vacation and school missed due to weather be calculated in how we identify late assignments?"

- "What if a student turns in an assignment that was due in the previous grading period? Do we still change the student's grade?"

In no way am I proposing that a person who legitimately challenges the details of a change initiative is a Fundamentalist. In fact, critical consideration of exactly what change would be most effective for students is typical of a Believer who is concerned about organizational effectiveness. A person who questions the wisdom of a school leader's decision is not necessarily exercising fundamentalism—he or she may have a very legitimate concern that deserves to be heard. The difference is that the Fundamentalists' objective through this line of questioning is not increasing or maintaining effectiveness, but obstructing change. It became very apparent to team members that the Fundamentalist teacher was not concerned about legitimate answers to her questions. Her goal was to create as many obstacles as possible to block the actual implementation of this or any strategy that would alter her practice. As the teacher who proposed the initiative answered each question the opposing teacher posed, it became clear that no answer was good enough to gain the Fundamentalist's compliance. The other two teachers on the team, both Tweeners, dared not challenge either the Believer or the Fundamentalist and stayed neutral. The teachers reached a stalemate, and the issue was eventually dropped, and no change in policy or practice was implemented.

In addition to this strategy of obstruction, Fundamentalists also try to make the case for avoiding change by identifying past ineffective attempts to solve a similar problem. Fundamentalists often try to represent coalitions that may or may not exist; they pretend as if they are the voice of many and thus have to step forward to speak for those who will not speak for themselves. Their message is this, "You may think you understand what the staff needs, but I know how the staff *really* feels." They might also share other schools' nightmare stories of attempts to implement similar initiatives. They try to paint a picture that says to the change agents, "This does not work, and everyone knows it except you."

Distraction

The last and least powerful method of resistance is distraction. When Fundamentalists realize that they cannot stop the change agent or the change initiative, they begin to display passive-aggressive behavior that articulates to the rest of the staff that they are being forced to change, and they do not agree or like it.

These behaviors include nonverbal communications such as rolling their eyes, assuming a negative posture, and engaging in an unrelated activity (like grading papers) during the planning or implementing of change. They will also freely share negative comments. When all viable avenues to blocking change appear to be closed, Fundamentalists retreat into a covert form of personal resistance. This form of resistance has no observable effect except to annoy others in the organization as a form of protest. In the study, Fundamentalists exhibiting this behavior usually complied with organizational decisions for change, but they were not willing participants. Schools that seek a healthy school culture and embrace change as a strong part of that healthy culture can deal with Fundamentalists at this level. These strong school cultures articulate the fact that behavior is more important than disposition. "It is good if you intellectually and emotionally embrace the critical change," they say, "but it is more important that you practice the change."

A Necessary Evolution

Fundamentalists pose the biggest and most critical challenge to schools seeking to create a healthy school culture. Their political stance is rooted in their perception that change is the enemy, and they organize to protect their very narrow view of how schools should operate. Leaders in 21st century public schools and beyond must realize that change is an inevitable part of organizational evolution. Those who are not poised to evolve and meet students' ever-changing needs they serve are doomed to eventually fail.

Education is too critical to our society for leaders to allow a group of individuals who refuse to embrace substantive change to hijack it, even in the face of compelling evidence. Fundamentalists might not have malicious intent, but their actions threaten to stunt the growth of the schools that serve our most needy students. School leaders and the Believers in our public school system have to become more active and vocal and meet this challenge of overcoming fundamentalism head on. In the next two chapters, we will take a look at real solutions that may curtail or eliminate fundamentalism altogether if applied properly.

CHAPTER 7

"Drop Your Tools": A Lesson in Change and Our Best Chance at Eliminating Fundamentalism

The primary problem in a toxic school culture is an inability to properly respond to challenges and adversity. Educators in such a culture become stagnant, and their stagnation can be the catalyst for regression. Fundamentalists' resistance to change maintains the status quo when schools should be ahead of the curve and actively seeking strategies that will allow them to fulfill their ultimate goal to the best of their ability: universal student achievement.

So in their attempt to evolve and develop a productive school culture without staff division, schools must consider two key questions.

1. What is the right change for us to embrace?

2. How do we get all staff members to embrace this change and actively apply the right methods once we have identified them?

In *Good to Great*, Jim Collins (2001) calls the process of answering these questions *getting the right people on the bus*. Stephen Covey (2013) describes this process as *synergy*, which combines the words *synchronization* and *energy*. According to Covey (2013), when all an organization's members have their missions and purposes aligned and combine that alignment with energy, they create a powerful force.

If people who lead businesses and other organizations understand and embrace these concepts, why don't school employees embrace the same concepts and set the standard for organizational effectiveness? No industry has more on the line than education. If we are going to produce better and more prepared students, school culture must become aligned in purpose and collective focus on student achievement. Anything less than a unified effort will continue the trend of falling short in our goal for students.

DuFour et al. (2008) sum up the challenge of aligning paradigms and operating under the synergy that Covey (1989) advocates:

> Contemporary educators are being called upon to fulfill a new purpose—high levels of learning for all students. . . . To meet that challenge, educators must do more than write catchy mission statements; they must align the structures and cultures of their institutions to support their new mission. They must act in new ways. (pp. 115–116)

Taking into consideration the various political agendas of the four groups identified in this book, especially the Believers and Tweeners, how can school leaders accomplish this synchronization and solidarity of focus necessary to create powerful schools? To find this answer, I would like to use a concept I call *educational pathology*.

Pathology is the scientific study of the nature of disease and its causes, processes, development, and consequences. As an education concept, *pathology* demands that a change agent carefully study the origin of a particular problem first to gain a clear understanding of its development. Once a leader has traced the origin of the problem, the solutions to the problem become clear. This strategy makes the leader look deeply into the root of the problem so that reactions will not be surface level and solutions will not be short lived. The leader will be able to clearly ascertain the conditions that caused the problem and the mentalities that may have contributed to it. This concept assumes that holistic examination and complete understanding of a problem will lead to focused and effective solutions.

We can use educational pathology in our quest to eliminate the effects of fundamentalism in our school culture by examining the very nature of organizational resistance. We must consider the following questions.

- Why do people resist change?

- What conditions motivate people to change?

- How can leaders create the conditions that would motivate people to accept change?

There is no study more qualified to explain the conditions that prevent people from changing than the *drop your tools* research (Weick, 2009). This research examines firefighters' reactions during two significant forest fires: (1) Mann Gulch in western Montana and (2) South Canyon in Glenwood Springs, Colorado. Both these fires resulted in high numbers of firefighter casualties. Though their supervisors gave the firefighters direct orders to "Drop your tools and run!" many firefighters chose not to run, even though there were clear opportunities to change course and save their own lives. In this study, Karl Weick (1996) poses two questions.

1. Why is change so complex?

2. Why would a person refuse to change at the risk of losing his or her own life?

Weick (1996) thought that if we could understand why a person would reject change in the face of grave danger and ignore the first law of nature—survival—then we could understand the root of all resistance to change. Weick's work in this area provides powerful insight into human resistance to change.

The first of the two disasters, Mann Gulch, was made famous in Norman Maclean's (1992) book *Young Men and Fire*. The accident occurred on August 5, 1949, when fourteen young smokejumpers, their foreman Wagner Dodge, and a forest ranger were trapped near the bottom of a 76 percent slope in western Montana by an exploding fire. Thirteen of these men were killed when they tried to outrun the fire, ignoring both an order to drop their heavy tools and an order to lie down in an area where fuel had been burned off by an escape fire. Dodge survived by lying down in the cooler area created by the escape fire, and two others, Bob Sallee and Walter Rumsey, lived by squeezing through a break in the rocks at the top of the slope.

At South Canyon, outside Glenwood Springs, Colorado, a similar event occurred forty-five years later on July 6, 1994. Again, it was late on a hot, dry, windy afternoon as flames lit the side of a gulch as firefighters moved onto steep slopes and into dense, highly flammable forest to fight the fire. A wall of flames quickly raced up the hill toward the firefighters. They could not outrun the flames, and twelve firefighters perished (Weick, 1996).

In both cases, the firefighters who perished did not drop their tools or packs while trying to escape. Dropping their tools or packs would have significantly increased their chances of escape. An analysis at Mann Gulch concluded that had they dropped their packs and tools, they could have moved more quickly while exerting the same amount of energy, and two analyses of the events revealed that "the firefighters would have reached the top of the ridge before the fire if they had perceived the threat from the start" (Maclean, 1992, p. 134).

Inspiring Fundamentalists to Drop Their Tools

What possible lessons can we learn from these two tragic events? First and foremost, Weick (1996) points to the fact that they were both very preventable. The firefighters who perished did not have to die. Their resistance to guidance and their unwillingness to change their course, even when the evidence before them was overwhelming, reveal the ultimate case of fundamentalism. After examining the evidence at these two tragic events, Weick (1996) identifies four key reasons why the firefighters did not drop their tools, and he rates the intensity of resistance from level one to level four based on the reason or rationale for resistance: (1) having communication, (2) building trust, (3) building capacity, and (4) having accountability. His research provides key insight in the fight to get Fundamentalists to "drop their tools" and seek a more productive methodology. Fundamentalists in our schools also display varied levels of resistance that are directly related to their reason or rationale for adopting the fundamentalist paradigm, so we will not only identify their reasons for resistance, but also rate their intensity from one to four, with one being the weakest and four being the strongest.

Level One Fundamentalists (Why?—Having Communication)

People persist when they are given no clear reasons to change.
—Karl E. Weick

What makes Level One Fundamentalists? They resist change because they were never provided with a clear rationale for change. They resist because they simply do not understand why they need to change. They need to understand *why* they need to change. This means that leaders can either avoid or reverse resistant behavior when they develop *communication*. Weick (1996) illustrates this concept in his explanation of the trouble at Mann Gulch and South Canyon:

> Foreman Dodge did little briefing of his crew throughout the incident. One of the few times he spoke to them was when he gave the order to drop their tools. When the accident investigation board asked Dodge to tell them what reason he gave for dropping tools, Dodge replied, "It wasn't necessary. You could see the fire pretty close and we had to increase our rate of travel some way or another." What was clear to Dodge may not have been as clear to the other 15, nine of whom were first-year smokejumpers and all of whom had more experience fighting fires in timber than in the dry grass where they now found themselves. At South Canyon, the firefighters who kept their tools were also not given a reason to drop them. No one told them that they were at the head of an onrushing fire, which is crucial information, because it was plausible for them to perceive that they were on the north flank of the fire. (p. 48)

The leaders of the fire crews at both Mann Gulch and South Canyon made critical mistakes at crucial times. They assumed that the firefighters saw things the same way they viewed them and understood facts and realities that they never formally explained. Simply because leaders understand the context and urgency of a situation does not mean that their followers share the same perspective. Leaders must share information on a regular basis, and followers must clearly comprehend it before compliance can be expected.

In a study of human cooperation, Terence Burnham and Dominic Johnson (2005) provide some valuable insight on understanding Level

One Fundamentalists. Burnham and Johnson (2005) find that human beings resist cooperation when their cognitive need to understand is not fulfilled. This is human nature: the human psyche works against blind cooperation and seeks a logical explanation before charting an unfamiliar course. Therefore, a Level One Fundamentalist's needs are legitimate. They resist change, and will continue to resist change, until their need for a logical explanation is met. These findings provide great hope for influencing the behavior of Level One Fundamentalists and recruiting them to the ranks of Believers.

What do these findings tell us about administrative or leadership behavior? They teach us one critical lesson: *The absolute worst way to change human behavior is by creating an illogical mandate strictly on the basis of coercion.* An analysis of 21st century educational policies would show us that this methodology has been used regularly and with very little effectiveness in the late 20th and early 21st centuries. No Child Left Behind and ESSA, despite their noble goals, were introduced in this manner. Schools were told to improve student test scores immediately or face punishment. There was no logical case presented to the educators who had to implement this policy. It was introduced to the entire educational community as a blanket mandate. Educators were ordered to improve student performance without an explanation about why student performance needed to be improved. The methodology chosen to introduce the change created new Fundamentalists rather than reforming existing Fundamentalists. In fact, an entire sector of the education community came together to fight NCLB. Educators resisted the initiative because they were not provided with a clear reason to embrace this sweeping paradigm change.

Education leaders at the district and site levels cannot repeat the mistakes of the federal and state governments. They cannot simply expect compliance from their subordinates because they can order them to make a change. School leaders must first make a clear and solid objective case for change before expecting people to embrace the change. Educators must appeal to the sense of service with which most educators enter the field as Tweeners. Leaders can use some of the following information to make a solid, objective case for change.

- Data and statistics that create a catalyst for change in an inspirational way, instead of in a threatening way

- Empirical research that paints a clear picture that a technique or strategy is more effective than the one currently practiced

- An organizational mission and vision that give a rationale for adapting a potentially more potent strategy

Level One Fundamentalists can be easily converted. The basis of their resistance is logical and easily fixed. Leaders must resist the urge to boss or coerce their way to change. Change is best and permanent when a meeting of the minds occurs and the change is intrinsic as opposed to extrinsic. When leaders start to clearly articulate rationale and fulfill their staff members' need to understand, they can quickly move these Fundamentalists to new levels of productivity in our school culture.

Level Two Fundamentalists (Who?—Building Trust)

People persist when they don't trust the person who tells them to change.

—Karl E. Weick

Level Two Fundamentalists resist change because they do not trust the leader's judgment or skills. They question the leader's credibility, which in turn causes them to distrust the credibility of the leader's guidance. People are not likely to change if they do not have confidence in the person *who* is leading them through the change. This means that resistant behavior can either be avoided or reversed when a leader develops the skill of *building trust*. Weick (1996) explains how this concept played out during the Mann Gulch and South Canyon fires:

> Members of the firecrew at Mann Gulch did not know Dodge (the squad leader) well, which made it hard for them to know how credible his orders and actions were. At South Canyon, the Prineville firefighters did not know the five smokejumpers mixed in with their crew, all five of whom had told the crew either to run or to deploy their shelters. In the eyes of the smokejumpers these instructions were not legitimate orders, nor were they mentioned by trusted people. (p. 49)

Level Two Fundamentalists develop a general distrust of school leaders that may or may not have anything to do with current leaders. They tend to express their distrust in their leaders' motivations in the following ways. They think:

- School leaders are motivated by looking good and moving up the career ladder

- School leaders are untrustworthy, making promises to please others instead of providing honest feedback based on reality

- School leaders are hungry for power and seek to dominate teachers

- School leaders do not understand the modern teacher's plight and are too far removed from the classroom conditions to be effective

All these issues develop out of an experience or series of experiences that caused the Level Two Fundamentalists to adopt this perspective. If school leaders hope to move Level Two Fundamentalists from fundamentalism to belief in the possibility of universal student achievement, they must bridge the trust gap. This trust gap has two key components: (1) leader competence and (2) character.

The leadership research is very clear when it comes to the correlation between effective leadership and trust. The U.S. Army identifies what they refer to as the *twenty-three traits of character* necessary for a person to effectively lead in the armed forces (U.S. Department of Defense, 1973). There is no place where snap decisions and alignment between leader and subordinate are more important than on the field of battle, where every decision can mean the difference between life and death. Even under these extreme circumstances, leaders must be more than just knowledgeable; troops have to trust them before they will follow a leader's commands.

The United States Army's 23 Traits of Character	
1. Bearing	13. Will
2. Confidence	14. Assertiveness
3. Courage	15. Candor
4. Integrity	16. Sense of humor
5. Decisiveness	17. Competence
6. Justice	18. Commitment
7. Endurance	19. Creativity
8. Tact	20. Self-discipline
9. Initiative	21. Humility
10. Coolness	22. Flexibility
11. Maturity	23. Empathy or compassion
12. Improvement	

Source: U.S. Department of Defense, 1973.

The business community is also very clear on the effects that the leader's character have on the productivity of an organization. *The Walker Loyalty Report for Loyalty in the Workplace* notes that trust, especially in leadership, is the single biggest factor in worker retention (Baldoni, 2007). The report goes on to cite several ways managers can boost their trust level with their employees. The strategies include:

- Do not make promises that cannot be kept.

- Back your people when it counts.

- Take responsibility and be publicly self-reflective when times are tough.

What can a school leader do to develop trust as the bridge to organizational health? First, he or she must realize that the Level Two Fundamentalist has a legitimate need for trust. If trust has been breached through a series of experiences, the resistant teacher will not move from his or her position until that need has been met. School leaders must remember that, in many cases, the emotional gap that Level Two Fundamentalists display may not be a direct result of anything the leader has personally done; rather, it may be the result of a collection of bad experiences in the past that the current leader must fix. It may seem unfair, but the Level Two Fundamentalist's need still exists, and the school culture is held hostage until that need is met.

Trust is broken in the eyes of the Level Two Fundamentalist when he or she questions the character and competence of a leader. To bridge this gap, the leader may consider the following strategies.

- Hold regular and public celebrations for both teachers' and students' accomplishments.

- Stay away from the limelight, and exhibit true humility.

- Do not violate rules he or she expects others to follow and for which the leader holds them accountable.

- Frequently use the pronoun *we* when publicly discussing the school's accomplishments or future plans.

- Make good on his or her word. The leader should do what he or she promises to do.

- Do not ostracize Fundamentalists for holding different opinions. Guarantee them their right to their opinion in a way that preserves their dignity, even if the leader philosophically disagrees with them.

In the area of competence and trust, a school leader may bridge the gap in the following ways.

- Know his or her stuff! Stay well-versed in the evolving knowledge base of education.

- Lead teachers in the learning process. Expose them to knowledge that enlightens their practice and gives them a new context.

- Familiarize him- or herself with the history of the school and community, and articulate a vision that will inspire others to think in new ways.

- Continue to improve his or her skills and credentials. Nothing says competence like a person who exhibits the quality of lifelong learning.

Level Three Fundamentalists (How? — Building Capacity)

> *People may keep their familiar tools in a frightening situation because an unfamiliar alternative is even more frightening.*
>
> —Karl E. Weick

Level Three Fundamentalists are educators who resist change because they are unsure if the change will cause them more stress, and perhaps still not achieve a better result than their current methodology. They have real doubts about their ability to produce the desired outcome, so they wrestle with the concept of accepting the *devil that they know* in exchange for the *devil that they don't know.* People are less likely to change when they don't possess a high level of confidence in the change, and they do not know *how* to effectively implement the change. This means that leaders can avoid or reverse resistant behavior when they develop *capacity building.* Weick (1996) shares the following analysis of the events at Mann Gulch:

> People at Mann Gulch found it hard to drop their tools, but they found it even harder to comprehend the function of Dodge's escape fire. No one followed Dodge (the leader) in, and some thought the fire was supposed to serve as a buffer between them and the oncoming blowup. It is equally strange to be told to deploy a fire shelter. Firefighters do not get much practice deploying fire shelters. Furthermore, it is tough to open a shelter while running in turbulent winds, with gloves on, and while looking for a clear flat area in which to lie down. (p. 51)

In stressful situations, people make tough choices, and the firefighters were no different. They had to decide between using methodologies that were familiar to them, even though the odds did not appear to be greatly stacked against them, or try a strategy that was new, complicated, and untested. This dilemma is familiar to teachers. To effectively move Level Three Fundamentalists into cooperation with Believers, leaders have to address two issues: (1) proper preparation and (2) incremental implementation of change.

People are more likely to embrace change when they are properly prepared for change. Many public schools are in a situation similar to the one the firefighters found themselves in at Mann Gulch. Many educators are bombarded with various change initiatives that neither make sense nor strike a particular chord. They are being asked to consider many possible alternatives while managing a sundry of responsibilities that occupy the vast majority of their time. Investing time, a rare and precious commodity for educational professionals, on all of the various reform initiatives that come across the principal's desk can have a numbing effect on educators. The constant need to put out fires and deal with issues that Stephen Covey (2013) calls *quadrant 1 issues*—issues that are *urgent and important*—leaves little time to seriously consider the adoption of *quadrant 2 issues*—issues that are *important but not urgent*. According to Covey (2013), growth is gained in quadrant 2. When important issues are properly researched, pondered, and developed—without the anxiety and stress of urgent time-consuming factors—the quality of the developed ideas is much better than the ideas or decisions made in quadrant 1. Quadrant 2 decisions impact overall operations in a profound way, and perhaps reduce the number of quadrant 1 issues. Simply put, when people get a chance to think before they act, their decisions are much sounder.

School days are filled with important and urgent issues. Effective administrators will make progress with Level Three Fundamentalists when they make time for personal and professional growth for all teachers. The firefighters at Mann Gulch had a very limited perspective on change. The chief's commands were unfamiliar and ill-placed. Expecting people with very little professional development and growth opportunities to make critical decisions on important issues while simply trying to survive is not a good way to encourage change. In fact, many of the Fundamentalists I interviewed mentioned their frustrations with all of the varied change initiatives that they were forced to adopt. They complained of little to no training and no consideration from administration for all of the daily duties that were still their responsibility.

For a Level Three Fundamentalist, developing capacity and skill in an environment that is conducive to cognition will make meaningful change much more likely when potentially powerful opportunities for growth are presented. Richard DuFour and Rebecca DuFour (2006) describe professional learning communities (PLCs)—environments conducive to cognition that make meaningful change possible. They note that "PLCs operate under the assumption that the key to improved learning for students is continuous job-embedded learning for educators" (p. 2). They describe the growth of educators as the catalyst for their students' growth. This growth has to be job-embedded, which supports the idea of quadrant 2 development that Covey (2013) advocates.

While serving as principal at Levey Middle School in Southfield, Michigan, I led my staff in what became known as the *learning center concept* (Buffum et al., 2008). The learning center concept was an ongoing and daily system of growth and development in critical areas of need for our teachers. This system poised my staff for change through intentional exposure to new ideas that would provide the cognitive framework for accepting the right change at the right time. The learning center concept had the following characteristics.

- **Data driven:** A team of educators examined our critical data to determine important areas of need. This also helped provide a rationale for change for our Level One Fundamentalists.

- **Founded on relevant research:** The team of educators found relevant literature and research that supported growth in critical areas of need. Teachers were provided this information in advance and invited to participate in intellectual discourse.

- **Contextual:** Leaders were concerned about the teaching staff's tremendous daily workload, so they employed the concept of *addition by subtracting* by eliminating traditional staff meetings and instead dedicating that time to professional growth. No new time requirements were added to the teachers' load to facilitate a proposed activity.

- **Collaborative:** Teachers were placed in very diverse teams of study partners in which they could problem solve and share insights.

The opportunity to interact with various schools of thought in a nonthreatening way on an ongoing basis opened many teachers up to the possibility of change who otherwise would have been closed to the idea. The environment and frequency of the learning centers eased their anxiety and prepared them for future school experiments that would make a real and transformational difference for their students. The engagement was gradual and ongoing so teachers did not feel they had to change course all at once. Improvement was focused on the long haul as opposed to short bursts of desperation.

Level Four Fundamentalists (Do!—Having Accountability)

> *People may refuse to change because change may mean admitting failure.*
>
> —Karl E. Weick

The last reason the firefighters refused to drop their tools gives insight to just how complex change can be for Level Four Fundamentalists. Level Four Fundamentalists pose a particularly puzzling problem. There is not a lot that leaders can do to change their paradigm because they have defined themselves within the organization by their resistance to change. To drop their tools and cooperate, they would have to redefine themselves to the other members of the organization. Level Four Fundamentalists are so deeply rooted in their opposition to change that it consumes and defines them. They have no real observable needs except to be defined by their political position within the school. Weick (1996) describes this reason for resistance at Mann Gulch and South Canyon:

> To drop one's tools may be to admit failure. To retain one's tools is to postpone this admission and to feel that one is still in it and still winning. Finally, implicit in the idea that people can drop their tools is the assumption that tools and people are distinct, separable, and dissimilar. But fires are not fought with bodies and bare hands, they are fought with tools that are often distinctive trademarks of firefighters and central to their identity. Firefighting tools define the firefighter's group membership, they are the firefighter's reason for being deployed in the first place, they create capability, they are given the same care that the firefighters themselves get (e.g., tools are collected and sharpened after every shift), and they are meaningful artifacts that define the culture. (p. 52)

Weick's (1996) argument is that some of the firefighters never planned to retreat, regardless of their circumstance. To run from a fire would be to redefine their purpose as firefighters. Firefighters are defined by their bravery and the willingness to run into the teeth of danger and save others. Running, and even more important, dropping the tools that were the symbols of their ability to save would undermine their own self-concept, therefore identifying them as failures. These firefighters would not have followed the commanders' request to retreat under any circumstances. According to Weick (1996), the only way that the firefighters would have dropped their tools and retreated is if they were physically dragged out of the fire. Under no conceivable circumstance would they have chosen this option on their own. Some people are not compelled to change unless there is a true demand for performance and a system in place to ensure that they do or perform the task for which they have been prepared. This means that a leader can avoid or reverse teachers' resistant behavior when they develop *accountability*. Therefore, there is only one real solution for Level Four Fundamentalists: strict monitoring. Leaders must send the message that the standards have changed, and the only way someone will be allowed to be comfortable is through compliance with the new school paradigm.

The skillful school leader should be able to effectively employ the strategies outlined in this chapter to significantly transform the paradigms of the Level One, Level Two, and Level Three Fundamentalists. Once the transformation takes shape at these levels, leaders should be able to isolate the Level Four Fundamentalists and use monitoring and coercion to force a change in behavior or a change in scenery. The illogical resistance of Level Four Fundamentalists will eventually call leaders into a battle of will. This is a fight that the school leader must win, because to allow Level Four Fundamentalists to operate in a school culture in the midst of effective transformation is akin to sanctioning the behavior. School leaders who understand that their true purpose is to lead an organization dedicated to service on behalf of students will not blink when this showdown arrives.

The monitoring tools available to leaders vary from place to place, but every school leader has some formal system to closely monitor unproductive and uncooperative employees. These tools generally include a trail documenting a teacher's performance to either assist with improvement or to help with termination of employment if performance does not improve. In many unionized states, this process is bargained, so the school leader must be careful to follow the mandated system of monitoring explicitly outlined in the master agreement. I have seen many administrators start down this road of formal monitoring of uncooperative teachers only to have the process interrupted or eliminated because of a loophole or a policy that was not followed properly. Where these agreements exist, school leaders must be very careful to make sure that the requirements of the master agreement have been satisfied. In areas where these agreements do not exist, leaders must be careful to make sure that whatever the district considers to be *due process* is honored and followed. The best case is that the mere presence of a formal monitoring system creates a level of discomfort and anxiety in a Fundamentalist, which will cause the Fundamentalist to focus on his or her own behavior.

School leaders often have the right of teaching assignment; they have the power to determine who teaches what and to whom. In many of the cases I observed in my study, Fundamentalists sought and often occupied coveted teaching positions in schools, like teaching honors classes, while many Believers and Tweeners were assigned to much more challenging positions. Most significantly, leaders must place Level Four Fundamentalists in positions in the school where they are likely to do the least amount of harm to students. Refusing to even consider change in critical educational practices may create academic gaps in essential areas of development, like mathematics and reading. The exposure to this subpar practice may cause a student to struggle for years to come as he or she becomes exposed to deeper levels of rigor in other grades and courses. One principal I observed in the study placed Level Four Fundamentalists in a generic "support" class called Study Skills until he applied enough pressure for the very ineffective and stubborn teacher to either quit or change. Second, assigning them to coveted positions sends the message to the rest of the staff that the behavior of the Level Four Fundamentalists is acceptable. A principal in one middle school involved in this study removed a Fundamentalist from his position as the social studies department chairperson and assigned him to a generic study skills class. The Fundamentalist was replaced in his chairmanship with a Believer, and the drastic change in working conditions caused him to quit and seek a position elsewhere. This may seem somewhat cruel or coercive, but the principal articulated to me that disappointing his former teacher was much more acceptable than disappointing his students, parents, and progressive staff members.

Ending Division

Good leadership is important. As I've seen, Fundamentalists tend to behave the way they do due to their reactions to bad leadership. When educators become accustomed to leaders who fail to communicate, build trust, properly prepare them for a task, and hold everyone accountable, it is easy to understand why a person would gravitate toward Fundamentalist behavior. I encourage leaders to view Fundamentalists as a mirror of their leadership. The behaviors that leaders see in others are usually manifestations of how they have affected those that they lead. A leader's job is to transform and positively impact behavior, and when leaders improve, culture improves.

Leaders understand that their behavior makes a significant contribution to their schools, districts, families, communities, nation, and world. Leadership is serious business. An ineffective leader can make a lasting negative impression; and an effective leader can positively impact lives for generations. Every school and district deserve transformational leaders. Transforming school culture requires four very essential skills that are imperative for a leader to become a transformational leader. Transformational leaders are:

1. **Skillful communicators**—People tend to resist change to practice and lack motivation to improve when leaders have not skillfully communicated the rationale or case for improvement. If teachers are going to embrace a vision, they have to clearly understand the vision and feel personally compelled to contribute to it.

2. **Trust builders**—The ability to connect with others' emotions is a very essential skill of a transformational leader. People aren't just inspired by facts and objective evidence, they also need to connect with their leaders on a personal

level and know that leaders are not only intellectually connected to their purpose but also ethically connected.

3. **Capacity builders**—People are more willing to take a risk and try a new idea if leaders have prepared them professionally. Investment in training, resources, and time is essential if we want educators to enthusiastically embrace new ideas and practices.

4. **Results oriented and courageous (accountability)**— Ultimately, improvement cannot be optional. A transformational leader must skillfully assess and meet his or her subordinates' needs, but eventually he or she has to demand full participation in the change and improvement process.

The good news is that Fundamentalists can be reformed and redirected in most cases. Level One Fundamentalists simply seek clarity in matters that involve changing long-held practices. School leaders can accommodate their requests very easily. Level Two Fundamentalists have an emotional need. Their experiences have created a general distrust of school leadership. A combination of exhibiting trustworthiness, ethics, humility, maturity, and patience can heal the very real wounds that Level Two Fundamentalists have and change their behavior for the better. Level Three Fundamentalists are uninformed, stretched, and overwhelmed. When leaders regularly address their knowledge gap, they provide a framework for not only understanding change, but eventually embracing it. Level Three Fundamentalists also need to see the long-range picture, and steady change spread over time works best for them as they struggle to deal with the myriad of responsibilities that hits them on a daily basis. Level Four Fundamentalists reject change because it potentially can redefine them and identify them as failures. Their goals are more important to them than those of the school, so leaders must use the tools at their disposal to hold them responsible for meeting new organizational standards.

This idea of producing synergy or getting the right people on the bus is not an easy one, especially for schools. Schools have limitations that businesses and other organizations do not have. Schools cannot simply terminate people who do not cooperate with their goals and replace them with more suitable professionals. Legal and employment regulations do not allow that. Creating healthy cultures in schools is a difficult endeavor, but it can and must be done. My hope is that this new framework can raise the likelihood that we can effectively win this battle and create the kind of school cultures that embrace and nurture our young people.

CHAPTER 8

Implications for Practice

When analyzing organizations, especially schools, it becomes clear that meaningful and productive growth is primarily a function of the cohesion of human resources. Technical or structural changes can certainly aid this process, but if the human factors are not healthy, growth and transformation become very difficult. This book has made a case for understanding why schools have such a difficult time changing when members of the culture cannot accept new paradigms that do not mesh with the traditional operation of schools.

Unfortunately, many school leaders find themselves underprepared to deal with all the diverse aspects of school leadership, especially as it pertains to developing a healthy school culture (DuFour, 2001). This chapter will focus on practical methods that both administrators and teachers can use to loosen the grip of their Fundamentalists, overcome staff division, and focus the school on its primary purpose: student learning.

The schools I studied that were able to create and maintain a healthy school culture had some similar traits. They were all able to eliminate human distractions and call their colleagues to a higher, more professional purpose. This chapter will focus on six areas for action within schools and districts.

1. Developing a systematic and schoolwide focus on learning

2. Celebrating the success of all stakeholders

3. Creating systems of support for Tweeners

4. Removing the walls of isolation

5. Providing intensive professional development

6. Implementing skillful leadership and focus

Developing a Systematic and Schoolwide Focus on Learning

Richard DuFour (2002) characterizes most ineffective schools as disorganized and unfocused institutions without a set of clear and focused goals. The schools I observed with the most toxic cultures demonstrated that assertion. A 1989 Northwest Regional Educational Laboratory (now Education Northwest) report identifies the most observable and effective leadership strategy in effective schools with healthy cultures (Cotton, 1989). In these schools, leaders "framed school purpose policies in terms of one or two universal academic goals, which can in turn provide the framework for all other school activity" (Cotton, 1989, p. 71). This report also identifies the turning point for transforming school culture: the change process begins with the tone of the relationship between the leader and teachers, which then trickles down to affect the relationship between teachers and students. In order to influence student learning at the classroom level, the school leader must first demand that the organization as a whole focus on student learning. Education Northwest (2013) also supports this process.

DuFour et al. (2016) assert that the first big idea of a professional learning community is a focus on learning. They explain that highly effective schools accept student learning as their school's fundamental purpose. Leaders who are highly effective are skilled at focusing the entire organization on this purpose. DuFour et al. (2008) also point out that PLCs not only focus on effective classroom methods for improving student learning but also consider the learning of all school members as the catalyst for improving student learning. DuFour and Eaker (1998) note that the first characteristic of a PLC is developing shared mission, vision, values, and goals. They explain this process in the following manner:

> The mission question challenges members of a group to reflect on the fundamental purpose of the organization, the

very reason for its existence. The question asks, "Why do we exist?" "What are we here to do together?" and "What is the business of our business? (p. 58)

Schools that want to produce a healthy learning environment must first and foremost be clear about their collective purpose. As I observed in many schools, progress becomes nearly impossible without a collective commitment to service for the purpose of universal student achievement. The following sections will provide some practical strategies for developing this collective focus on purpose and its effect on school culture.

A Collective Focus on Purpose

During my study, I observed school staffs that were united in purpose. Some of these schools had long ago developed their positive and productive cultures, and some were in the beginning stages of development. They all shared some common traits.

- Staff members used a common vocabulary when articulating matters of student expectations and classroom methods.

- Staff members engaged in problem-solving conversations and universally shunned complaints.

- Staff members exhibited a high level of efficacy where the school mission and purpose were concerned.

I recall one particular faculty meeting that was specifically focused on the school's fundamental purpose. The principal was concerned that the school mission and vision statements were simply dogma and had no effect on the practices within her school. She led an activity with her staff that spanned three staff meetings and ended with a clear and universally accepted direction and mantra for their school.

As an experienced practitioner, I was not surprised that many of the staff members—especially the experienced ones—were not excited. This type of activity was not uncommon to many of them. Some revealed that on several occasions with past school administrators they revamped the mission statement, but such work proved to be an exercise in futility. Many complained that the exercises of the past were purely symbolic and had no real effect on day-to-day practices. They articulated three major problems with the mission debates of the past.

1. The prior attempts were unorganized. Leaders simply asked staff, "What do you think our mission statement should say?"

2. People with strong opinions quickly dominated conversations. Anyone who challenged their opinions had to engage in an unproductive argument, which made the activity more divisive than cohesive.

3. No substantial changes occurred after weeks of painstaking arguments.

However, it soon became clear that this meeting was unlike any other the staff members had experienced.

This principal's series of exercises was different for several reasons. First, the principal clearly stated the activities' purpose up front: "We want to get on the same page so that we can make sure that our students are successful." She clearly articulated the research on cohesive school staffs and their effect on student achievement. This may seem simple, but the problems that arise from lack of articulation of goals between leadership and subordinates are well documented. Organizations that move cohesively have established solid lines of communication that allow them to be more flexible and responsive to the needs of the organization (Wynn, 2006). Educators who become accustomed to the negative impact of "Do as I say" dictatorial leadership that has dominated schools in the past seem to embrace this type of transparent, collaborative leadership.

Second, she provided an accurate profile of the school's current performance as well as both educational and demographic data on the correlation between school performance and future life success. She created a compelling case for looking at alternative methods by demonstrating the failure of past paradigms and practices. Laying out the indisputable case for improving student performance put a human spin on the process. She was able to take the focus off of the teachers and their personal and individual needs and create an atmosphere that allowed them to collectively focus on what was best for the students.

After providing a compelling case for change, the principal divided the staff into discussion groups. Each group was armed with a comprehensive set of both achievement and demographic data on the students and community they served. She asked the discussion groups to consider the following four questions.

1. "Who are our students?"

2. "What strengths do they bring to the school?"

3. "What needs do they bring to the school?"

4. "How can we collectively enhance their lives?"

Before releasing the groups for their collaborative discussions, she established a very clever set of group norms. She instructed the groups to eliminate the following phrases from their discussions about school direction.

- "I think . . ."

- "I feel . . ."

- "I believe . . ."

Her rationale was that a decision as important as re-establishing the school's very purpose should not be subjective. If staff members were going to advocate for a particular focus or direction for the school, they needed to provide comprehensive data to make an objective case. These very clever additions to this process totally transformed the direction of the conversation when compared to similar activities conducted in the past. The principal and her assistant principal informally monitored the group discussions to ensure that groups followed activity guidelines, but offered very little input into the discussions.

This activity produced dialogue in ways that this school had never experienced before. Not only was the staff able to develop a cohesive and concise mission statement for their school, their dialogue prompted them to develop a three-year action plan focused on real change strategies that embodied their public statement of purpose. This renewed and uniform focus on purpose developed new energy among staff members. The language the staff used was noticeably different. The principal changed school policies and procedures that were not in alignment with their new mission. The staff also decided to sponsor a parent night where they articulated their new mission statement and plans for the next three years and asked parents to be partners in this process.

The school principal sought to define the purpose of her school around student academic achievement, and she was successful. She involved her entire staff, and staff members clearly took ownership in the process and voluntarily did things that coercion or manipulation could never accomplish.

Effect on School Culture

The focus of this school's mission activity was apparent: focusing all stakeholders in the organization on student achievement. The principal accomplished this end, but how did this affect the culture?

This activity, along with similarly structured activities, provided a strong catalyst for change for Level One Fundamentalists. These Fundamentalists resist change simply because they do not understand the rationale. This activity started with a complete and compelling presentation on the real effects of education in a student's life. Students who do well in school overwhelmingly succeed while those who do not complete school (or struggle in school) overwhelmingly lead painful and unproductive lives. The principal appealed to the heart of her educators. Her introductory activity sent this message: "If you were inspired to join the field of education to change the world, it is not going to happen under our current system." For Level One Fundamentalists, rationale means everything. When they understand, they cooperate.

This approach also gives Believers a platform to articulate their belief systems. One of the only problems with Believers is that they do not challenge Fundamentalists nearly enough to make a difference. In fairness to the Believers, in most schools, they are not given a platform to challenge those belief systems on a regular basis. Fundamentalists work well within the informal organization, and Believers may find that conversations in the teacher's lounge or during lunch are not the best places to wage an intellectual debate with Fundamentalists.

Structured meetings and activities provide Believers with solid data and empirical evidence to back their belief system, and formal rules keep conversations focused on the stated objectives. In the meetings I observed, a structured format made it very difficult for Fundamentalists to seize control over the collaborative discussions.

In addition, this activity gave Tweeners an opportunity to regularly reconnect with the very reason they chose the profession: to help students. With all the various new and stressful activities thrust on Tweeners, they can be easily overwhelmed and lose focus and purpose. Tweeners also enjoy hearing about and benefit from the expertise and experience of their colleagues. In the meetings I observed, Tweeners felt like they were a real part of the team, and the group activities served to humanize their colleagues with whom they did not have many opportunities to interact otherwise. The Tweeners found this process to be invigorating; it reinforced their rationale for choosing their career path. Simplifying and unifying the school purpose made the transition to the profession more palatable for new educators. It did not take away the stress of adjustment to all the varied and complex tasks involved in their jobs, but it made the challenges seem more worthwhile.

Celebrating the Success of All Stakeholders

Celebrating success has long been debated in the leadership arena. Many traditional thinkers believe that workers are paid to do their jobs, so therefore they should execute their responsibilities without fanfare. They think meeting job-related goals is just a part of the job, and celebrating expected achievement is unnecessary and even counterproductive. On the other hand, an emerging body of literature asserts that human behavior is complex, and celebration or appreciation for prowess on the job is one of the best and smartest ways to improve worker productivity (Amabile & Kramer, 2011). Studies have indicated that things like salary and opportunities to advance are very low motivators, but recognizing achievement and celebrating goal attainment are much more powerful methods for increased productivity (Chamorro-Premuzic, 2013). This school of thought does not view celebratory strategies as unnecessary fluff; rather, it considers celebration essential to human performance.

Celebration in school provides consistent reinforcement about what is important. People often celebrate what they value, such as holidays and birthdays, for example. How schools celebrate learning and those who help students learn says a lot about how much the school values learning. Lee G. Bolman and Terrence E. Deal (1995) describe organizational celebration in this way:

> Ritual and ceremony help us experience the unseen webs of significance that tie a community together. There may be grand ceremonies for special occasions, but organizations also need simple rituals that infuse meaning and purpose into daily routine. Without ritual and ceremony, transitions become incomplete, a clutter of comings and goings. Life becomes an endless set of Wednesdays. (p. 82)

The positive school cultures I observed consistently celebrated the things the school valued. These celebrations were both planned (or institutionalized) and impromptu, and all were authentic. Recognition was genuine and not manufactured for the sake of giving the appearance of false appreciation in the midst of low productivity. These schools set clear expectations for all stakeholders—students, teachers, administrators, support staff, and parents. When these expectations were met, the achievements were celebrated proudly and publicly.

Institutionalized Celebration

One elementary school I observed in my study found a very authentic and inexpensive way to consistently celebrate the attainment of its school goals. This school held staff meetings after school twice monthly and gave awards at each meeting.

The school gave *mobile awards*—trophies symbolizing prowess in one of four areas: leadership, curriculum, child advocacy, or creativity. The principal originally distributed the awards, and the recipients could keep and display their awards for two weeks. At the next staff meeting, the winners passed the honor on to a fellow staff member whom they observed exhibiting the quality that the award recognized.

Each staff meeting ended with passing the award from one staff member to another. The presentations were sometimes dramatic and sometimes emotional, but they were always authentic. The principal at the school had found a way for staff members to show genuine appreciation for one another in a public way that reinforced the school's goals and produced a spirit of teamwork necessary to build a high-performing school.

Other benefits of this activity are subtler, but even more powerful. By giving staff members a forum to speak positively about their colleagues, the principal was subtly changing a norm. Fundamentalists thrive in a culture of slander and defamation. If they can keep colleagues and leaders at bay by creating a culture of personal mistrust, their maintenance of the status quo has a fertile environment to prosper. When people start to trust one another and focus on service to students, they become more willing to accept change. In fact, they begin to embrace changes for the benefit of their students and are more willing to take risks both pedagogically and organizationally. It is hard for Fundamentalists to stir up feelings of contempt and distrust when their colleagues show such genuine appreciation for one another on a regular basis.

The other subtle benefit was changing the focus in the school from looking for the negative to looking for the positive. Human beings are creatures of habit; once we develop a habit, it is hard to break. Members of toxic cultures develop habits that breed consistent fighting and contempt. Members of a healthy culture consistently look for ways to validate their efforts. By turning over the responsibility of recognizing achievement to the staff, the principal forced them to look for positive attributes of their colleagues instead of looking for the negative. If a staff member received a leadership award, he or she had to spend the next two weeks looking for the best example of leadership among the other staff members. Repeating this activity over the long term caused a real transformation in culture. Looking for the positive was now the norm.

Impromptu Celebration

Not all the celebrations were planned and institutionalized. I observed several impromptu celebration strategies that sent messages that were equally clear. Many of these celebrations recognized student achievement as well as staff accomplishments.

In one high school, students received a variety of recognitions for accomplishments that ranged from improving test scores to being prompt for a particular class for an entire week. This high school developed what it called the *goodie jar*. A large jar was placed in the staff lounge and filled with donations that the school secretary and counseling staff gathered from the community, businesspeople, school store, athletic department, and principal. Some examples of goodies include the following.

- Professional sporting tickets (professional sports teams' donations)

- Passes to school events (both athletic and social)

- Certificates for free items (local business donations)

- Student privilege opportunities (free student parking passes, for example)

The items could be given to either students or fellow staff members, and the distribution was totally left to the staff's discretion.

The school secretaries, who organized and maintained this effort, had one rule: the jar must be empty by the end of each week. If they noticed by midweek that the jar was still full or nearly full, they sounded a collective alarm. They sent a barrage of emails, memos, and verbal notifications that more recognition had to take place. One secretary told me, "We have great kids, and they do great things every day, and they will not continue to show us their great side if we do not show how much we appreciate them on a regular basis."

Celebration and Positive School Culture

The schools that celebrated authentically on a regular basis created a great atmosphere for collegiality. Collegiality is not collaboration, but having colleagues who genuinely like and respect one another creates an atmosphere ripe for collaboration.

Consistent celebration provided the Believers with a comfortable school atmosphere. They felt at ease and more connected with the other members of the organization because they felt as if their paradigm was the prevailing one. Many of the Believers in the study who worked in healthy school cultures consistently mentioned the many celebratory aspects of their school and how recognizing proficiency and effort made them feel at ease and produced a sense of family.

Tweeners also benefited from the celebrations. Much of the recognition went to students and skilled veteran colleagues, but this did not seem to bother Tweeners. The celebration of success inside and outside of the classroom helped the Tweeners see what the future held for them. It helped them realize that the current struggles that many of them faced were not permanent and that education is not a collection of depressed and disgruntled professionals. Many Tweeners mentioned the joy they felt seeing their students recognized on a regular basis, and they could identify their colleagues as professional role models because of the public recognition they received.

Fundamentalists seemed to benefit from celebration as well—especially Level Two Fundamentalists. The catalyst for Level Two Fundamentalists' resistance is a void in their trust of leaders. The leaders who celebrated regularly and authentically started the process of reshaping Level Two Fundamentalists' view of leadership's role in the school. Because celebrations were authentic and all-inclusive, the leaders were indirectly building trust with more skeptical staff members. Fundamentalists are pessimistic about the likelihood of ever serving under an ethical and selfless leader, so leaders' willingness to honor others in selfless celebrations projects an image of high moral character that Fundamentalists yearn to see.

Creating Systems of Support for Tweeners

Effective school leaders, especially those managing high numbers of new teachers, must work very hard to properly develop and retain their Tweeners. Focusing attention on those with potentially influential contributions paid off for some of the effective school leaders I observed. These school leaders made a conscious decision to put the majority of their energy into properly grooming their new teachers as the catalyst for turning their toxic school culture into a healthy one over time.

A 2008 NEA report identifies new teacher mentor programs as one of the most vital aspects of building and sustaining powerful public schools (as cited in Moire, 2008). The report points out that the most effective new teacher mentoring programs have several facets. For example, simply assigning one mentor and assuming that the one mentor can meet the new teacher's diverse needs is probably not the most effective method. Rather, schools that are comprehensive and thorough and involve several members of the school community in the mentoring process are most effective at retaining and guiding new teachers.

In addition to not having the entire school community's support, new teachers often feel the isolation of the classroom. No other professional faces this unique isolation. For most of their professional lives, teachers will be the only adult in their immediate area of practice. This can be hard for veterans, and it can be fatal for new teachers. One new California teacher states, "Beyond problem solving and professional development, new teachers' experiences can be enhanced simply by being connected to a friend" (Christensen, 2008, p. 1). This teacher felt the impact of daily professional isolation and created an online community for new educators as a virtual support system for one another. I observed several effective leadership strategies during this study that controlled for the isolation factor and connected new teachers to support systems in innovative and effective ways.

Finally, effective school leaders developed systems that intensely developed the skill level of their new teachers in ways that limited their struggles in the classroom and in the school in general. These leaders felt that if they could shorten the learning curve for their new teachers and help them experience success in the classroom, these teachers would be less likely to suffer from many of the hardships that most new teachers experience. They achieved this goal in two different ways.

First, they made it acceptable to struggle and to seek help. In many of the toxic cultures observed, it was unacceptable to struggle. Struggle was a sign of incompetence, and the incompetent teacher drew the scorn of his or her supervisor. Consequently, these schools maintained a very high rate of teacher turnover. The effective schools publicized the fact that all professionals struggle, and they encouraged new teachers to articulate their struggles so that the school system could have firsthand information in order to assist new teachers with their transitions.

Second, effective school leaders developed meaningful and adequate professional development for new teachers focused on the areas in which new teachers struggle most. A program set up in Baltimore, Maryland, focuses on new teachers' real and critical needs (Baltimore City Public Schools, 2016). The program serves sixteen hundred new teachers participating in the Baltimore City Public Schools' New Teacher Summer Institute, a comprehensive three-year program for newly hired teachers. Started in 2006, the program provides hands-on lessons and much-needed support for new teachers. The program includes a comprehensive summer *boot camp* for new hires, followed by a New Teacher Summer Institute, and professional learning and site-based monitoring for teachers in years one through three. After one year of implementation in 2007, the district experienced a 30 percent increase in teacher retention (Lewis, 2006). In 2016, the program currently boasts a three-year retention rate of 63 percent, much greater than the national average of 41 percent after three years (personal communication, T. Jabonowski, April 28, 2017). The intensive program provides practical strategies in a variety of areas, including lesson planning, preparation, and instruction; the creation of student portfolios; classroom management and discipline; and communication with parents. The schools I observed used similar strategies, and they retained and empowered their new teachers as the catalysts for their school's cultural transformation.

Some schools in this study felt that the traditional method of pairing a new teacher with one veteran mentor teacher was not adequate to strengthen their Tweeners' performance. Two school principals and an associate superintendent identified new teacher development and retention as their top administrative priority. Their personal commitment and allocated resources were much higher than the other school leaders observed in this study. They felt as if it was the entire school community's responsibility to embrace and develop newcomers. One elementary principal stated that teacher failure is worse than student failure, "When one student fails, that one student suffers, but when one teacher fails, thirty students fail."

One elementary school in the study formed a *new teacher committee*. This committee consisted of the principal, three veteran teachers (all identified as Believers), the school counselor, and the main office secretary. Each committee member served a specific purpose in developing all the probationary teachers in the school.

The principal was responsible for the formal evaluation and pre- and postevaluation conferences for each Tweener. The veteran teachers played a unique role. Each was selected for a particular skill that distinguished him or her among the other teachers in the school. One was a master organizer, and her role was to work with all the new teachers in the area of organizational skills. She guided them in everything from developing powerful and organized lesson plans to completing grading requirements for students. The second teacher was known as a master at creative pedagogy. She had done extensive research on learning styles and multiple intelligences and could take any lesson and make sure all student learning styles were being addressed. She modeled lessons for the new teachers and met with each teacher one on one on a weekly basis. The third teacher was master at student relations and discipline. He was well-known by students and teachers as the teacher who connected best with students. He worked with the new teachers on classroom management. The counselor met with new teachers to coordinate support service needs, and the secretary made sure the new teachers stayed informed and did not drown in paperwork.

This system was extremely effective. Over the next seven years, this elementary school had a phenomenal retention rate of 100 percent. Many of the Tweeners I interviewed at this school identified the committee as a powerful influence in their development. They also mentioned how their associates at other schools who did not receive this type of support were now looking to move to other professions.

Removing the Walls of Isolation

The second big idea of PLCs is for schools to develop a culture of collaboration (DuFour et al., 2008). The powerful paradigm that we are much more effective together than we are separately drives the entire PLC process. Among the school leaders I observed, those who were most effective in this area were students of the PLC model, and they organized their schools into collaborative teams of teachers.

One high school principal was very methodical about how he assigned teachers to teams, especially new teachers. He had previously served as an assistant principal at another high school that was not quite as careful about how it assigned teachers to teams and how it monitored that process. He found that assigning teachers to unhealthy teams could produce more unhealthy teams. So when he became principal of his current school, he was careful how he exposed his new teachers. He made sure that new teachers were assigned to teams with a healthy and productive collaborative culture, instead of exposing them to less collaborative teams that might reinforce a culture he was working to change.

Teachers at this school were given two days per week to meet with colleagues during the school day in collaborative teams. On Tuesdays, teachers were assigned to content-specific teams. The subject department chairperson led these team meetings, and the agendas regularly included issues related to curriculum, assessments, instructional material, and pedagogy. On Thursdays, the veteran teachers met with other veteran content teachers to develop common formative assessments and review critical data. Simultaneously, the new teachers met with the department chairperson who advised them in all critical areas and allotted them time to ask questions without their veteran staff members present. This private collaboration made Tweeners comfortable with expressing frustrations and difficulty without the burden of judgment from the administration or veteran teachers. These collaborative sessions were very open and honest. Participants appreciated this opportunity, and many expressed that they looked forward to these weekly sessions.

This high school, like the elementary school identified earlier in this section, developed an excellent record of retaining new teachers. The principal began his tenure in 2002, inheriting thirteen probationary teachers and hiring eleven more. In 2017, the principal is the superintendent in the same school district. Of the twenty-four new teachers under his leadership when his tenure as principal began, seventeen are still teaching at that school, six are school administrators, and one left the profession to pursue other interests. These new teachers evolved from novices to the shapers and messengers of the school norms or accepted the challenge to lead and change other environments as administrators.

Providing Intensive Professional Development

One middle school principal in the study, a once-struggling new teacher himself, developed an intensive new teacher–development program at his school. This principal who once struggled with things like classroom management, lesson planning, and parent and community relations admitted that these struggles almost drove him away from the profession. He admits that informal sessions with a teacher who taught in an adjacent classroom saved his career. The informal sessions were like a series of informative workshops on what he called "how to survive until you can thrive in the classroom." He vowed that if he became an administrator, he would never let new teachers struggle to learn basic things that all good teachers should know. He did not want his new teachers to be trained by happenstance; he wanted them to experience an *intentional* system of development.

This school leader starts this system early on—in fact, it is part of the new teacher interview process. He and his hiring team make sure they articulate to a prospective new teacher that he or she must be a learner as well as a teacher. Candidates who do not display a willingness to be perpetual learners are not considered for employment.

Once new teachers are hired, they must attend onsite professional development every two weeks after school for one hour. These sessions are called *new teacher basic training*. The principal takes advantage of this military theme, weaving it throughout the language and promotion of the series. The topics for the sessions include:

- Having effective classroom management
- Administering standardized testing
- Implementing the curriculum and standards
- Understanding the school system and how to get things done
- Understanding what constitutes good homework
- Communicating with parents
- Taking time for personal interests and development

School staff who have developed effective methods in each topic area teach the courses at the school. They are paid a financial stipend to teach the course. The program has grown from three sessions in 2001 to eighteen sessions in 2017. This system brings the best out of both the new teachers and the veteran teachers, and the focus is on learning.

Supporting Tweeners empowers the Believers in a formal sense that gives them an official platform to push their paradigm. Socialization of new teachers is not left to chance. The most effective Believers are given the time and opportunity to mold the new teachers in the belief systems that support the fundamental purpose of the school. The staff members who participate also display a proud swagger; they feel their productivity and commitment to the school goals are valued. The Believers in these schools, compared to others, are more willing to challenge Fundamentalists both in the formal and informal organizations.

Tweeners obviously benefit from these approaches. They have access to the experts in the school—not by chance, but by design. Not only do they receive guidance through modeling, but they also are systematically provided with time to ask impromptu questions and receive guidance by the teachers in their school who perform best in the most important areas of teaching.

This system causes Fundamentalists to lose valuable access to the driving force of their movement: impressionable Tweeners. This system restricts access to the Tweeners in the formal realm, which leaves only the informal. Tweeners interviewed at these schools made little mention of recruitment efforts by nonmentor staff members in informal situations. Fundamentalists were curious about what took place during the mentor-mentee sessions, but had little to no effect on the guidance and advice given from the Believers. The Believers in these schools provided the Tweeners with enough good guidance that even when they had their *moment of truth*, the trust and confidence gained during regular mentoring and professional development sessions gave them the confidence to seek the advice of the building-assigned experts, instead of seeking the guidance of a seemingly empathetic Fundamentalist.

Implementing Skillful Leadership and Focus

Transforming a toxic school culture marked by significant staff division into a healthy one does not happen by luck. Skillful leadership and a focus on key areas of school operation are critical to this process. A focus on learning, institutionalized celebration, and new teacher development are great places for school leaders to begin the quest for improved school culture. This chapter provides a research base and practical strategies that have been successful in reshaping school culture. As school culture improves, students have a much better opportunity to learn in an environment that supports the practices that guarantee them a chance at success. The type of success they will enjoy will not be limited to just school; their success in the classroom will be the catalyst for their success in life.

CHAPTER 9

Frequently Asked Questions

Since the release of the first edition of *Transforming School Culture* in 2009, I have received hundreds of emails and messages full of questions about school culture, the Transforming School Culture framework, and education in general. I replied to all questions and saved them. Many questions were similar, so I paraphrased them and the answers in this chapter. The questions and answers focus on school culture, leadership, Believers, Tweeners, Survivors, and Fundamentalists.

I want this book to provide a mirror for the education profession and force people to question the status quo. Change and improvement are inseparable. I am grateful to all the people who have read this book and took the time to sincerely seek answers to their questions, even the questions and feedback that were slightly challenging.

School Culture

The following questions and answers are associated with general inquiries about school culture and its impact on school performance.

Q: What responsibility do parents and students have in building school culture?

A: Parents and students certainly affect school culture, but their role in shaping it pales in comparison to the educators who practice in that environment. Parents can use their power to lobby and advocate for advantages for their children, and this can create a dilemma in the school environment. "Helicopter parents" who try to influence their children's course selection, teachers, and grades can create an environment of politics if not kept under control. Parents who are totally aloof and disconnected can contribute to a general culture of low expectation. Parents who are hostile can produce a culture of fear or intimidation.

Students who are engaged and enthusiastic certainly improve the school culture. Students who are obedient and kind create a friendly climate and environment and better conditions for professionals to practice. Students who possess profound background knowledge bring a lot of skill and experience to the learning process. Conversely, students who lack background knowledge and are hostile toward their teachers and school in general significantly affect the school culture.

Parents and students play a major role in developing school culture, but they do not have nearly the effect that educators have. As cited in chapter 1 (page 25), John Hattie (2012) proves that *collective teacher efficacy* has a very strong and positive influence on student learning. I believe that the question posed is the wrong question. I would ask, "How can we influence parents and students to participate in building school culture?" This question places the agency with the professionals, who are the most stable part of the culture because parents and students only stay for a prescribed amount of time. When the question is focused on influence, rather than concern, a whole new world of strategies and practices becomes apparent. Strong cultures positively influence parents and students; they do not passively wait for parents and students to become more positively influential.

Q: Can an educator simultaneously fit into all four groups (Believers, Tweeners, Survivors, and Fundamentalists) in the Transforming School Culture framework?

A: No. The four subcultures are based on the educator's *objective*, not the observable behavior. For instance, many people automatically associate resistant behavior with Fundamentalists. This is a false assumption. A Believer can be legitimately resistant to change. A Believer's objective is *success for every student*. A Fundamentalist's objective is to *maintain status quo*. The objective is the constant, and the behavior is the variable. A faculty can be presented with a change initiative based on concrete student data. A Believer can legitimately resist because he or she does not believe that the proposed change is best for students.

The Fundamentalist will resist because he or she does not believe that it is personally beneficial. Resistance is a behavior, not an objective. What categorizes a professional on the Transforming School Culture framework is his or her objective, and the objective drives the behavior. If a professional wants to understand where he or she currently fits within the framework, then he or she should examine the motivation behind his or her behavior.

Q: How long does it take to transform a culture?

A: There is no standard time frame for transforming a culture. There are many factors that contribute to a culture's health or toxicity. In chapter 1, I shared Kent Peterson's definition of *healthy school culture* in two parts: (1) an unwavering belief that all students can and will learn and (2) a willingness to change practice in order to produce learning for all students (as cited in Cromwell, 2002, p. 4). So, if you are to transform your school culture, the first step would be to examine your school's collective beliefs and access your school's willingness to change behavior to improve student learning. Every school does not have the same starting point, so the transformation period will be different from school to school.

Another important factor in transformation is the school's willingness to embrace the behaviors of a healthy culture. Imagine if two people are sick with the flu, and they both visit the doctor. The doctor orders them to two weeks of bed rest and a special diet rich in vitamin C and antioxidants. One follows the doctor's instructions for two weeks, and the other patient follows the doctor's orders for two days. Who is most likely to heal faster? In chapter 7, I outline four critical behaviors that leaders need to adopt in order to positively transform a culture: (1) communication, (2) trust building, (3) capacity building, and (4) accountability. If these behaviors are fully acted on and integrated into a school's culture, obviously culture will develop faster. If they are partially implemented or totally ignored, a toxic school culture could linger forever.

Q: Wouldn't our school cultures be healthy if we just got rid of high-stakes testing?

A: Certainly high-stakes testing, a cornerstone of the Global Educational Reform Movement, has adversely affected school culture, but culture problems did not begin with GERM. Low student expectations, poor graduation rates, and hostile school environments did not start with high-stakes standardized testing. My K–12 school experience was hostile. We felt that many of our teachers did not care for us personally, and this resulted in constant teacher-student conflict, high suspension rates, and a low graduation rate. This all occurred before NCLB or ESSA. The roots of a healthy culture are a collective passion for student success and a willingness to be the agent of student success. A culture of testing and punitive accountability measures adds an additional degree of difficulty, but it would be disingenuous to declare that they are the sole culprits. Most of what it takes to transform a school lies squarely within the locus of control of the educators that work in that environment.

Leadership

The following questions and answers focus on leadership.

Q: How can we develop a healthy culture when our school has a very high principal turnover rate?

A: It is very difficult to sustain momentum when the direction of the school or system is constantly changing due to attrition at the leadership level. If schools and districts are serious about transforming culture then careful selection, development, and retention of leaders is important. In chapter 4 (page 57), I address the importance of Tweeners in the development of school culture. High turnover in that group is detrimental to the school's long-term development. It undermines instructional consistency and organizational memory. In chapter 8 (page 119), I describe several schools and districts that developed and maintained a healthy culture by systematically supporting new teachers. My advice would be that schools and districts place the same premium on supporting leaders.

I would like to caution any teacher reading this answer from dismissing himself or herself from responsibility for this problem. I would encourage you to be your best advocate! If leadership turnover has been a calumny at your school, gather your colleagues and speak with the authority about the type of leader that you desire, then actively engage in the process of finding, supporting, and retaining a good leader. There is no benefit to simply criticizing a reality. It is more beneficial to use your ability to influence reality.

Q: How can we build culture when the district office gives us a new initiative or changes course every year?

A: It is very difficult to create a healthy culture and sustain momentum when the school or district changes focus consistently. This goes against everything that we know in our field about sustained progress (see DuFour & Marzano, 2011; Marzano & Waters, 2009; Schmoker, 2011). System leaders cannot be reckless enough to take their employees on an annual roller coaster ride of change (also known as the "flavor of the month") and then still expect them to be enthusiastic about embracing change. School and district leaders have to do a better job defining critical objectives, collaboratively engaging with professionals, and implementing a long-term plan to achieve school and district objectives. If school and district leaders do not get strategic in their approach to change and abandon the flavor-of-the-month approach, their cultures will remain toxic and ineffective.

Q: What if your leader is a Fundamentalist?

A: If your leader is a Fundamentalist, that is the worst-case scenario. A Fundamentalist teacher can only use persuasion and informal influence. A Fundamentalist leader influences policies, structures, and resources. In the Transforming School Culture study, I witnessed Fundamentalist leaders who coveted the Old Contract of leadership, which was to be a good manager and keep the teachers happy. When they entered the profession, management proficiency and a happy staff were the benchmarks of success. A good principal was considered someone who attended all school functions, created positive relationships with parents and students, and provided the resources and support that teachers needed to practice autonomously. The current educational climate and political climate demand that a school leader focus on student learning outcomes and become an instructional leader. This transition did not meet the approval of some leaders who enjoyed the status quo of the Old Contract.

What I found was that Fundamentalist leaders and Fundamentalist teachers created an alliance. If the Fundamentalist leader protected the Fundamentalist teacher from substantive change, the teacher would in turn protect the leader's reputation, image, and security in private (informal culture). This alliance created a stalemate for change. Believers tended to be discouraged and in some cases bullied when advocating for a different direction. In this case, the only thing that I observed that was effective was strong intervention from the central office, with the board of education's backing. The central level of power was the only influencer strong enough to break the negative influence of a Fundamentalist school leader.

Q: How can I be an advocate for change when my leader refuses to hold Fundamentalists accountable for fully participating in the change process?

A: Accountability is a very important part of creating a healthy culture as chapter 7 outlines on page 112. Most Fundamentalist behavior is a response to bad leadership, and a leader's lack of courage places a Believer in a precarious situation. A Believer does not have the power to discipline a colleague, but Believers have the power of peer pressure. If there is synergy among a group of progressive teachers, and there is a Fundamentalist among you that is an outlier, those teachers have an obligation to bring their displeasure to the attention of their colleague. When an individual grossly disrespects the will of the group, silence becomes permission. If educators encourage students to voice their displeasure with a classmate exhibiting bullying behavior, it is certainly reasonable for educators to hold themselves to the same standard. Peer pressure may not work on every Fundamentalist, but it sends the message that his or her behavior is unacceptable in that environment. Peer pressure does not release leadership of its responsibility to create and enforce systems of accountability, but it does provide some temporary relief until you get a leader with courage.

Q: How can we build culture when my leader does not care about me and does not take time to know my colleagues or me personally?

A: Human beings have a natural need to connect to others. Relationships are very important to us. Unfortunately, everyone does not have an innate ability to develop personal relationships, including leaders. A person struggling with this issue should ask him- or herself, "Why do I have a need to feel close to my leader, and why is it a prerequisite to improving my practice?" As I establish in chapter 1 on page 19, there is a big difference between *climate* and *culture*. Climate is how we *feel*, and culture is how we *behave*. Professionals do not have to be endeared to each other in order to create a highly productive environment; they just have to get clear on their roles and responsibilities and faithfully execute a productive plan. It certainly helps if the individuals like each other, but it is not necessarily essential. So, I would advise anyone struggling with this issue to focus your energy on what you need from your leader in order to do a better job. Every person has the right to his or her personality, and as long as that person's personality does not adversely affect your ability to do your job, I would not place a lot of emphasis in this area.

Believers

The following questions and answers focus on the needs and concerns of Believers.

Q: How can a Believer gain influence in an environment that Fundamentalists dominate?

A: If you want to gain influence, stand on your moral and ethical truth. In chapter 7 (page 99), I explain that Fundamentalists thrive on emotion, and they struggle in the context of rationality. Do not allow Fundamentalists to bait you into a battle of emotions. If you want to influence them, do your homework and be prepared to clearly articulate why your proposal or theory is more rational than theirs. That's where Believers win.

Q: What do I do if I am experiencing Believer *burnout?*

A: Exchanges with people who are stubborn and often vicious can be emotionally and intellectually draining. I understand why many people choose *flight* over *fight* in these situations. But, if the objective of a Believer is success for every student, he or she cannot disengage. In fact, I found that Fundamentalists anticipate that their pessimism will ultimately extinguish the light of optimism, and once that happens, the culture is in serious trouble.

When Believers find themselves getting weary, think about this question: if Believer burnout exists, does Fundamentalist burnout exist? Have you ever witnessed a person who gets tired of being pessimistic? Neither have I. Why should Fundamentalists control the philosophical passion of the school? If Believers are truly student advocates, their advocacy should be more potent than the stubborn resistance of Fundamentalists. So, if pessimism can fuel an eternal flame of passion, shouldn't optimism be a better fuel? Never get tired of advocating for positive change. Your advocacy may be the difference in the future of the students in your school. Remember, we are architects of human potential and students' dreams. I cannot think of a more noble cause. So, put your "big boy" and "big girl" pants on, and march on!

Q: When I speak up against the Fundamentalists in my school, I get ostracized and bullied. What should I do?

A: When you considered education as a profession, what were your motivators? Love for your subject matter? Love for learning? A general affinity for children? I am sure that there were positive drivers that led you to the field of education. I am also confident that the admiration of your colleagues was not one of your drivers. Anyone struggling with negative attitudes and feedback from their colleagues who disagree with a stance or a stated opinion should remember that in mathematics the product of two negatives is positive, and the product of a negative and a positive is a negative. So, if negative people view you negatively; that's positive. If negative people view you positively; that's negative. I would argue that we spend too much time worrying about the arbitrary opinions of others, rather than being true to our authentic selves and our core values. Seeking approval of people who stand for everything that you disagree with says more about the person seeking approval than the people withholding the approval.

Tweeners

The following questions and answers focus on the needs and concerns of Tweeners.

Q: My mentor is a Fundamentalist. What should I do?

A: Tweeners are the most vulnerable members of our profession, and placing an impressionable new educator within the care of someone with negative influences is like exposing a baby to a dangerous virus before he or she builds an immune system. In chapter 8 (page 119), I explain that creating effective systems to develop and retain new talent is a cornerstone of developing new culture. New educators placed in this situation are victims of the dysfunction of the established culture.

Any Tweeners who find themselves in this situation need to seek the counsel and advice of someone that he or she can trust. Tweeners are vulnerable. In many cases, they do not have a lot of labor protection, and they are novices at understanding the power structure in their environment. If there is another teacher or colleague that you trust and respect, share your concern with that person and ask for his or her guidance. He or she can either help you find the right way to share your concerns with your mentor or your leadership or can speak on your behalf. All Tweeners need to seek a support system or network to help you navigate problems until you feel confident enough to do it on your own.

Q: How can a leader create a Tweener-friendly environment?

A: A leader's ability to recruit, cultivate, and retain new talent is an essential component of effective leadership. In chapter 4, I explain the *wall of silence*. Tweeners are vulnerable because they fear that their developing skill set, if exposed, can lead to their early dismissal from the profession. Conversely, many leaders mistake the cooperative nature of Tweeners with job satisfaction and contentment. This misunderstanding can lead to the *wall of silence*, where both parties operate off of assumptions and misunderstanding. A leader who wants to create a Tweener-friendly environment has to intentionally tear down that wall.

In order for Tweeners to feel comfortable, they have to understand that it's OK to make a mistake. Leaders have to carve out collaborative opportunities for Tweeners to share their troubles and concerns without fear of repercussion. Connecting Tweeners to the school community on a personal level is important as well. I was a college athlete, so coaching sports was the connection that I needed to make it through the rough patches in my early career until I had established more substantive roots. Leaders have to understand Tweeners' needs and the context in which they operate and be proactive in meeting these needs.

Q: I am a Tweener, and when I try to share my insight with my experienced colleagues, they disregard my input, and it makes me very uncomfortable. What should I do?

A: It is difficult to balance the dual task of respecting veterans and their knowledge and experience and giving voice to your ideas, especially when they contradict veterans. My advice has two parts. First, refrain from showing disrespect as a new faculty member, even if the conditions are frustrating. Secondly, find a way to acknowledge something positive about your environment before criticizing a practice or condition that others have grown to covet.

Sometimes, silence is golden. When a Tweener is trying to establish himself or herself as a valuable new addition to a culture, sometimes it's best to be silent in moments of disagreement and prove your point through your actions and the results that you achieve. Evidence is much more powerful than opinions, so when you choose to advocate for a different practice or direction, produce evidence, and let the evidence speak for you. When a person interacts with others in a new environment, the new member has to recognize that others do not have a history of interactions with you. Your first impressions create a profile of you that others will utilize for as long as you work in that environment. First impressions are powerful; don't blow the opportunity with arguing over things that may not be very important. Pick your battles carefully, and always make sure that you acknowledge good when you see it. It will allow others to receive your critiques more objectively.

Survivors

The following questions and answers focus on the needs, concerns, and impact of Survivors.

Q: How can a principal effectively address a Survivor in an environment with a strong teachers' union?

A: A principal must remember that a Survivor is an empathetic figure and the goal is to help, rather than to punish. I have never found a union that was opposed to its members getting help. In approaching the union, I would make the following three recommendations.

1. Acknowledge the systemic conditions that helped to create the current conundrum (such as lack of professional support, leadership turnover, and traumatic experience).

2. Meet with the district human resources department or an attorney before constructing a plan of assistance to present before the union.

3. Be prepared to produce data to support your claim that in his or her current state, the teacher is detrimental to himself or herself, students, and the school.

I have found that when leaders approach the topic of Survivors with an attitude of empathy and the spirit of assistance, they usually get a favorable response from the union. If that does not work, consult with the human resources department and legal counsel to start the dismissal process because the Survivor is adversely affecting students.

Q: What signs should I look for if I find myself spiraling into becoming a Survivor?

A: The best cure for any ailment is prevention. In chapter 5 (page 70), I outline some of the signs and characteristics of burnout. Some of those signs are high stress, hopelessness, and low energy. Some professional signs would be high frequency of *busywork* for students, misuse of technology, and student bargaining. If any, or all, of these symptoms start to become a regular part of your professional experience, act immediately. People who feel like they are spinning their wheels and falling into the abyss of professional depression have to understand that they are their best advocate. If you don't speak up, it can be very difficult for someone to help you, especially if you work in an ineffective culture. There are three ways that you can advocate for yourself and receive assistance before your situation grows into burnout.

1. Share your experiences with a colleague that you admire professionally and ask for direction.

2. Approach your leader with specifics concerning the issues that are bringing you down and your desire to overcome these obstacles.

3. Share your concerns with a union representative or teacher-advocacy group that can work with the school or district to provide you with the resources and support that you need to improve.

The worst thing that you can do is to do nothing. Once burnout starts, it can metastasize very quickly. Education is a very important field, but individual well-being is even more important. When a person is suffering psychologically, it not only affects him or her professionally, it affects those that the person loves. I always tell teachers, "Thirty years of depression is not worth a retirement check."

Q: How can I advocate for my own child if I feel that a Survivor is educating him or her?

A: One of the most important roles that a parent plays is an *advocate*. In a healthy culture, the entire faculty would serve as the student's advocate, but unfortunately, all students are not currently educated in a healthy culture. For example, if parents feel that their child is being educated in a fourth-grade classroom led by a Survivor, the first concern is that their child will only have one fourth-grade experience and that experience will shape their K–12 journey. The child's needs have to be more important than the teacher's feelings or the school's or district's reputation. But your approach should be factual and resolute and not emotional and vindictive. My advice to parents would be as follows.

- Gather as many artifacts and concrete evidence of poor instruction or non-instruction as possible (such as

assignments, ungraded homework, or free days), and take it
to the principal.

- When meeting with the principal, with evidence in hand,
  demand a follow-up response within a defined time
  parameter. Do not leave the principal's response open-ended;
  he or she may be a Fundamentalist.

- If the principal does not give you a favorable response,
  or he or she does not respond within the agreed-on time
  parameter, take your argument to the central office or board
  of education.

- Do not stop advocating until the conditions in the classroom
  change or your child has been placed in a classroom with a
  more capable professional.

Fundamentalists

The following questions and answers focus on the behavior and
impact of Fundamentalists.

Q: What if a Fundamentalist believes that he or she is a Believer?

A: It does not matter what a person believes he or she is; his or her
place on the Transforming School Culture framework is predicated on
the teacher's objective and his or her willingness to change to improve
the experience for students. I like to call a Fundamentalist a *me first*
as opposed to a *we first* individual. His or her personal desires are
consistently placed above the organization's needs. As a coach, it was
difficult to coach a player, no matter how talented, when his or her
personal statistics were more important than team aspirations. So, if a
person truly claims to be a Believer, watch how he or she reacts when
asked to make him- or herself uncomfortable (such as with standards-
based grading, common formative assessment, or reteaching a concept)
in exchange for a potential benefit for students. If such a person is willing
to change his or her behavior, and the educator can see the potential
benefit in taking a different direction, then he or she is a Believer. If
he or she is presented with evidence that a different course of action is
potentially beneficial for students, yet slightly more inconvenient for
the educator, and that person refuses to change despite the evidence,

then he or she is a Fundamentalist. The Transforming School Culture framework was not developed to be a personality assessment, it was designed for schools to have a mirror to assess their readiness for progressive change.

Q: If I disagree with the direction or ideas of my leadership, does that make me a Fundamentalist?

A: No, not necessarily. If you cannot bring yourself to embrace an idea after considering all the evidence, and you conclude it is not better for students, you not only have the obligation to voice opposition but also the responsibility to propose an alternative. If Jim Collins (2001) points out that change is stimulated by *confronting brutal facts*, it is acceptable to disagree with the response to those facts, but it is not acceptable to disregard the facts.

If a high school sets a goal of achieving 100 percent high school graduation for its students, yet currently only 70 percent of students graduate, that's a brutal fact. As your leader looks deep into the problem, he or she proves that a high student failure rate in ninth-grade mathematics is the biggest driver of student dropout. He or she proposes a mathematics support course for all ninth-grade students to address the failure problem. If you reject the idea simply because you do not want the inconvenience of providing additional support for struggling ninth-grade mathematics students, you are a Fundamentalist. If you reject the idea because you believe that the issue is not student support, it is poor instruction, and practice needs to improve at the classroom level, not with an additional hour of ineffective instruction, you are a Believer who has a different theory of improvement.

Q: How can a leader effectively transform a culture when he or she is experiencing the three Ds (defamation, disruption, and distraction) from their Fundamentalists?

A: Personal attacks and dirty politics can wear on the psyche of even the strongest person. What makes this dilemma even worse is typically the person advocating for positive change is an innocent victim of dysfunction that predates his or her arrival to that culture. When people feel comfortable defaming others, using personal relationships to influence decisions, and intentionally disrupting the implementation of change, those standards were probably established a long time ago! Chapter 6 (page 77) identifies that Fundamentalists thrive on conflict and emotion, and that is why they are typically the loudest and most vocal when it comes to advocacy. My advice to those victimized by these unsavory practices: stick to the following three methods.

1. **Defamation:** Be very mindful of your moral conduct. There are people who are waiting to destroy an idealist's momentum. Do not give people anything true to defame you with, and take the moral high road when you are falsely accused. Never let them see you sweat!

2. **Disruption:** Do no let Fundamentalists make you feel defensive like a badgered witness. If you have done due diligence in researching and articulating your proposed direction for your school, do not become upset when others challenge that direction. Challenge them to provide a better proposal and produce stronger evidence, and sit back and watch them crumble.

3. **Distraction:** Define and enforce professional standards, and model what you enforce. If timeliness is important, start all of your meetings on time and respond to people who are late. If full engagement is important, model that by being fully engaged in a professional learning activity with your teachers, and respond to people who are not engaged. If you don't want people to distract others from the norms, you have to model and protect them.

A leader may not be responsible for adverse cultural conditions that predated his or her leadership, but the leader is responsible for transforming the culture. As we have witnessed in politics, personal attacks and nastiness can create a sideshow that distracts all of us from the issues at hand. Effective leaders understand how to rise above the noise and model the behavior that defines what they claim to believe. My experience as a leader has put me in the crosshairs of people whom I had never harmed or for whom I had no ill will or intent. It tested every fabric of my being, but my willingness to persevere allowed me to connect with others of goodwill to create a learning environment that was effective and consistently beat the odds.

EPILOGUE

A Significant Impact

As a former teacher and administrator, I can appreciate the challenges that educators face on a daily basis. It is not easy to work with students from diverse backgrounds and value systems and still create the harmonious school ethos and shared value system that the public expects. But if we are to be a society that mirrors this expectation we have of schools—diverse, just, and harmonious—we must transform our public school system to accomplish this end.

The purpose of this book is to stimulate conversation and inspire educators to analyze the impact of their belief systems on their practices and how those practices impact their students. When students are nurtured in a culture where educators believe in their potential to do the extraordinary and work together to achieve this end, all students can be successful. This goal is hard to accomplish if the school staff is divided into four political groups with four different agendas. In a school culture where educators are aware of stereotypes, historical injustices, and the effects of being socialized in a class-based society, they are better prepared to create a healthy, nurturing environment for students—whether that school is located in an economically affluent suburb or in a housing project in an economically depressed inner city.

This issue is personal for me. I grew up in Flint, Michigan, in the 1970s. At the time of my childhood, Flint was a booming industrial center for General Motors. Employment opportunities were abundant, and the automotive industry fueled Flint's bustling economy. My home was right in the middle of a working-class neighborhood on the north end of Flint. When I was a child, the neighborhood was vibrant and alive with the laughter of children. I had four very close friends. We were inseparable, and we had hopes and dreams of becoming great one day and making our mark on the world. My friends came from very close-knit families that provided all the love and support that a young man would need. Their home was like mine, except for one very critical difference.

The parents of my close friends all worked at the various General Motors plants around Flint, except one mother, who was a homemaker. Of the seven parents that worked in the factory, only three graduated from high school, and the remaining four did not complete their high school education, yet the abundant opportunities offered by the automotive industry provided each household with a very comfortable, middle-class income. My mother was different in our neighborhood because she was the only person that did not work in the auto industry; she was a teacher in the Flint Public Schools. She eventually earned her master's degree in education, but despite her education, her income did not come close to matching an income from factory wages. So even though my mother was highly educated, we were poor compared to my neighbors.

This difference also set up a dissimilar set of expectations in school where achievement was concerned. The homes where my best friends were reared did not enjoy a middle-class lifestyle through the traditional means of using education as the vehicle for social mobility. Their income rose as a result of the prosperity of the American automotive industry, therefore there was not a connection between education and quality of life. All of my friends' parents valued education, as do the vast majority of parents regardless of social class, but they were caught in the mirage that the American automotive industry would always be prosperous and that their children would one day inherit their jobs. Their parents wanted them to do well in school, but there was no real sense of urgency where achievement was concerned. My home was very different. My mother set very high and rigid standards for school performance for my siblings and me. My mother demanded exemplary school performance.

My buddies and I all attended the same schools and were exposed to the same things at school and in the neighborhood. We were all ambitious and vibrant. There was no real difference in ability or intellect. We achieved in school at nearly the same level until about fourth grade. At that point, I was pushed on to an honors track, and they were on the average track. One of my friends was placed in special education. By high school, the differences were more pronounced, and I was a part of a very small group of honor students. By the end of high school, only three of us graduated. I was the only one of the group that went to college. Our schools presented us with opportunities for high achievement for those who were interested, but with the automotive industry at its peak, many of my classmates chose to drop out of school and go work in the factories. This was such a normal part of my city's culture that very few people inside or outside the school system seemed to be alarmed.

The culture that we experienced within our school walls sent different messages to us. There was a core group of Believers, which we appreciated, and they inspired us to achieve even though many students would not pursue advanced learning opportunities and would work in the factories. There were definitely Tweeners and pockets of Survivors, but the Fundamentalists were also present. Their social Darwinist characteristics discouraged many of my friends, and I personally witnessed discouraging and damaging commentary from them. They articulated in subtle and overt ways that the factory was our best option, and that that was just how the world worked. Many of us developed an animosity for these faculty members as well as a dislike for school in general. One of my friends quit high school because of this feeling of being unwanted because he did not fit the right profile.

In the mid-1980s, the American automotive industry took a major blow. Declining sales, rising costs, and foreign competition caused General Motors and other manufacturers to close plants and eliminate jobs. The jobs that my friends and their families thought would be there forever were gone. Plant closings in Flint came fast and furious, and my friends found themselves with very little education in a world with few job options. Today, two of my friends are no longer alive, one is incarcerated, and the fourth friend is trying to make ends meet through temporary employment. I have enjoyed an exciting career in education and have achieved even more than I could ever have dreamed as a child. Why is there such a difference in the trajectory of our lives? It is not because of abilities or greater intellect. I grew up in a healthy home culture where education was valued, and my education has been the foundation of my adult life.

This was not a prevailing paradigm in many of my friends' homes, and, unfortunately, not even in many of the classrooms that we attended as students in our local schools. My friends were left vulnerable to the ills associated with low academic achievement that chapter 1 outlined. This left a lasting impression on me. All students deserve a quality education despite their level of interest and parental involvement—this is an imperative in the 21st century and beyond. When human beings are at their best, they are thoughtful, ethical, productive, and humane, and a quality education can produce all these attributes. My greatest hope is that educators grasp this concept and universally dedicate themselves to creating schools that provide adequate guidance and support for all students and that schools aspire to become the transformational institutions that make the community a better place to live in and our world a better place.

APPENDIX

Study Design

The foundation of the Transforming School Culture framework is a result of the study identified in this appendix. The insights provided in the second edition are intended to provide an updated context for the findings of the original study to ensure that they continue to be relevant for years to come.

Sample

This study was conducted by collecting data from thirty-four public schools in the United States scattered across four regions—East, Midwest, South, and West. (See table A.1 on pages 158–159.) The study included eleven elementary schools, fourteen middle schools, and nine high schools. These schools ranged in student enrollment from small (200–400) to medium (401–1,000) to large (1,001-plus). Student socioeconomic status spanned poor (over 50 percent of students receiving free and reduced lunch) to moderate (10–49 percent) to affluent (9 percent or less). Student racial population ranged from diverse (more than two racial groups of 25 percent or more) to moderate (three or more racial groups of 10 percent or more) to homogeneous (one racial group comprising more than 90 percent of student population).

Data Collection

This study was an ethnography, and data were collected over a three-year period (2004–2007) using three methods.

1. Informal observations of classrooms in session during regular school hours, staff meetings, teacher team meetings, and other formal and informal gatherings of staff members were used to collect observational data.

2. Formal interviews were conducted with each building principal and a randomly chosen group of teachers at each school. Each interviewee was asked the same questions, and their answers were tape-recorded.

3. A document review was done at each site. These documents included student grade reports, student and staff attendance reports, and standardized test results.

The names of staff members and students were kept confidential on all reports the building and district administration provided.

Variables

This study examined two aspects of school culture: political objective and political motivation. The researcher used the data collected to determine the educator's objective or organizational goal through examining his or her interaction with all members of the organizations and correlating the observed behaviors with stated objectives during formal interviews and document and data reviews. The data collected were used to create a series of independent or predictor variables. Once the political objective or category was determined, the researcher sought to identify the educator's motivation through examination of literature and theory related to organizational behavior in currently published sociological literature. See table A.1.

Table A.1: Schools in the Study and Their Demographic Data

School	Region	Size	Socioeconomic Status	Racial Diversity
Elementary A	Midwest	Small	Moderate	Homogeneous
Elementary B	South	Medium	Moderate	Diverse
Elementary C	South	Small	Poor	Diverse
Elementary D	West	Small	Affluent	Diverse

Elementary E	Midwest	Small	Moderate	Moderate
Elementary F	Midwest	Medium	Moderate	Diverse
Elementary G	East	Medium	Poor	Homogeneous
Elementary H	Midwest	Small	Poor	Homogeneous
Elementary I	East	Medium	Affluent	Homogeneous
Elementary J	West	Small	Poor	Diverse
Elementary K	Midwest	Small	Moderate	Diverse
Middle School A	Midwest	Medium	Poor	Homogeneous
Middle School B	East	Medium	Moderate	Moderate
Middle School C	East	Large	Moderate	Moderate
Middle School D	South	Medium	Poor	Diverse
Middle School E	West	Medium	Poor	Homogeneous
Middle School F	Midwest	Large	Affluent	Homogeneous
Middle School G	Midwest	Medium	Moderate	Moderate
Middle School H	Midwest	Small	Poor	Homogeneous
Middle School I	South	Medium	Moderate	Diverse
Middle School J	West	Medium	Poor	Moderate
Middle School K	West	Medium	Moderate	Moderate
Middle School L	East	Large	Affluent	Homogeneous
Middle School M	Midwest	Large	Moderate	Homogeneous
Middle School N	Midwest	Medium	Moderate	Moderate
High School A	South	Medium	Moderate	Diverse
High School B	West	Large	Moderate	Moderate
High School C	Midwest	Large	Moderate	Homogeneous
High School D	East	Large	Affluent	Homogeneous
High School E	Midwest	Large	Poor	Homogeneous
High School F	Midwest	Medium	Moderate	Moderate
High School G	Midwest	Large	Affluent	Homogeneous
High School H	South	Large	Moderate	Homogeneous
High School I	Midwest	Small	Moderate	Diverse

References and Resources

Albert Shanker Institute. (2015). *The state of teacher diversity in American education*. Washington, DC: Author.

Allen, J. (2007). Inequality in funding of public education raises justice issues: Quality often depends on where students live. *National Catholic Reporter, 2,* 3.

Allen, M. B. (2005). *Eight questions on teacher recruitment and retention: What does the research say?* Washington, DC: Education Commission of the States.

The Alliance. (2016). *Every Student Succeeds Act primer: Accountability.* Washington, DC: Alliance for Excellent Education. Accessed at http://all4ed .org/wp-content/uploads/2016/12/ESSAPrimer-Accountability-FINAL .pdf on February 27, 2017.

Amabile, T. M., & Kramer, S. J. (2011). The power of small wins. *Harvard Business Review, 89*(5), 70–80.

The Annie E. Casey Foundation. (2011). *2011 KIDS COUNT data book.* Baltimore: Author.

Applied Research Center. (2000). *Facing the consequences: An examination of racial discrimination in the public schools.* Oakland, CA: Author.

Baldoni, J. (2007, October 3). *Leadership: Trust matters* [Blog post]. Accessed at www.fastcompany.com/blog/john-baldoni/grab-n-go-leadership/lead ership-trust-matters on October 27, 2008.

Baltimore City Public Schools. (2016). *Summer programming for newly hired teachers.* Accessed at www.baltimorecityschools.org/Page/25563 on May 8, 2017.

Bannister, R. C. (2008). Social Darwinism. In *Microsoft Encarta Online Encyclopedia.* Accessed at http://encarta.msn.com on October 27, 2008.

Bannister, R. C. (2010). *Social Darwinism: Science and myth in Anglo-American social thought.* Philadelphia: Temple University Press.

161

Barnes, G., Schaefer, B., & Crowe, E. (2007). *The cost of teacher turnover in five school districts.* Washington, DC: National Commission on Teaching and America's Future.

Barr, G. (2008). Study: Texas school system fosters low graduation rates. *Dallas Business Journal.* Accessed at www.bizjournals.com/dallas/stories /2008/02/11/daily36.html on October 10, 2008.

Bidwell, A. (2014, February 27). The history of Common Core State Standards. *U.S. News & World Report.* Accessed at www.usnews.com/news /special-reports/articles/2014/02/27/the-history-of-common-core-state -standards on June 12, 2017.

Bolman, L. G., & Deal, T. E. (1995). *Leading with soul: An uncommon journey of spirit.* San Francisco: Jossey-Bass.

Brown, K. M., & Wynn, S. R. (2009). Finding, supporting, and keeping: The role of the principal in teacher retention issues. *Leadership and Policy in Schools, 8*(1), 37–63.

Buffum, A., Erkens, C., Hinman, C., Huff, S., Jessie, L. G., Martin, T. L., et al. (2008). *The collaborative administrator: Working together as a professional learning community.* Bloomington, IN: Solution Tree Press.

Burnham, T. C., & Johnson, D. D. P. (2005). The biological and evolutionary logic of human cooperation. *Analyse and Kritik, 27,* 113–135.

Butler, J. A., & Dickson, K. M. (1987). *Improving school culture: School improvement research series.* Portland, OR: Northwest Regional Educational Laboratory.

Carnevale, A. P., Smith, N., & Strohl, J. (2010). *Help wanted: Projections of jobs and education requirements through 2018.* Washington, DC: Georgetown University, Center on Education and the Workforce.

Chamorro-Premuzic, T. (2013). Does money really affect motivation? A review of the research. *Harvard Business Review.*

Chang, W. H., Park, J. J., & Shim, S. (1998). Effectiveness of negative political advertising. *Web Journal of Mass Communication Research, 2*(1), 17.

Chiodo, A. J., Hernández-Murillo, R., & Owyang, M. T. (2010). Nonlinear effects of school quality on housing prices. *Federal Reserve Bank of St. Louis Review, 92*(3), 185–204.

Christensen, F. (2008, August 5). *New teachers: Alone in the classroom, together in the chatroom.* Accessed at www.cvc.edu/faculty/articles-opinions/posts /new-teachers-alone-in-the-classroom-together-in-the-chatroom on October 27, 2008.

Collins, J. (2001). *Good to great: Why some companies make the leap . . . and others don't.* New York: HarperBusiness.

Conley, D. T. (2014). *The Common Core State Standards: Insight into their development and purpose.* Washington, DC: Council of Chief State School Officers.

Cotton, K. (1989). *Expectations and student outcomes: School improvement research series.* Portland, OR: Northwest Regional Educational Laboratory.

Covey, S. (1989). *The seven habits of highly effective people.* New York: Free Press.

Covey, S. (2013). *The seven habits of highly effective people: Powerful lessons in personal change* (25th anniv. ed.). New York: Free Press.

Cromwell, S. (2002). Is your school culture toxic or positive? *Education World, 6*(2). Accessed at www.educationworld.com/a_admin/admin/admin275 .shtml on March 2, 2017.

Davis, J. H. (2015, December 10). President Obama signs into law a rewrite of No Child Left Behind. *The New York Times.* Accessed at www.nytimes .com/2015/12/11/us/politics/president-obama-signs-into-law-a-rewrite -of-no-child-left-behind.html?_r=0 on February 27, 2017.

DeWitt, P. (2016, February 3). *Why collaborative leadership matters most* [Blog post]. Accessed at http://blogs.edweek.org/edweek/finding_common _ground/2016/02/why_collaborative_leadership_matters_most.html on February 28, 2017.

Di Carlo, M. (2015). *Update on teacher turnover in the U.S.* Washington, DC: Albert Shanker Institute.

Dizon, N. Z., Feller, B., & Bass, F. (2006, April 18). *States omitting minorities' test scores.* Accessed at www.boston.com/news/education/k_12/articles/2006/04 /18/ap_states_omit_minorities_school_scores on October 27, 2008.

DuFour, R. (2001). Community: Getting everyone to buy in. *Journal of Staff Development, 22*(4), 3.

DuFour, R. (2002). One clear voice is needed in the din. *Journal of Staff Development, 23*(2), 4.

DuFour, R. (2015). *In praise of American educators: And how they can become even better.* Bloomington, IN: Solution Tree Press.

DuFour, R. (2016). *PLC at Work—ESSA: An opportunity for American education* [White paper]. Bloomington, IN: Solution Tree Press.

DuFour, R., & DuFour, R. (2006). The power of professional learning communities. *National Forum of Educational Administration and Supervision Journal, 24*(1), 2–5.

DuFour, R., DuFour, R., & Eaker, R. (2008). *Revisiting Professional Learning Communities at Work: New insights for improving schools.* Bloomington, IN: Solution Tree Press.

DuFour, R., DuFour, R., Eaker, R., Many, T. W., & Mattos, M. (2016). *Learning by doing: A handbook for Professional Learning Communities at Work* (3rd ed.). Bloomington, IN: Solution Tree Press.

DuFour, R., & Eaker, R. (1998). *Professional Learning Communities at Work: Best practices for enhancing student achievement.* Bloomington, IN: Solution Tree Press.

DuFour, R., & Marzano, R. J. (2011). *Leaders of learning: How district, school, and classroom leaders improve student achievement.* Bloomington, IN: Solution Tree Press.

Earl, L. M., & Katz, S. (Eds.). (2006). *Leading schools in a data-rich world: Harnessing data for school improvement.* Thousand Oaks, CA: Corwin Press.

Education Northwest. (2013). *Leading school improvement with "intension"— lessons learned.* Portland, OR: Author.

Feller, B. (2006, April 20). *AP poll: Teachers dubious of 'No Child.'* Accessed at www.highbeam.com/doc/1P1–122146681.html on October 27, 2008.

Ferguson, R. (1998, April 7). Teacher perceptions and expectations and black-white test score gap. In C. Jencks & M. Phillips (Eds.), *The black-white test score gap* (pp. 273–317). Washington, DC: Brookings Institution Press.

Friedman, T. L. (2005). *The world is flat: A brief history of the twenty-first century.* New York: Farrar, Straus and Giroux.

Fullan, M. (2003). *The moral imperative of school leadership.* Thousand Oaks, CA: Corwin Press.

Fullan, M. (2011). *Choosing wrong drivers for whole system reform* (Seminar Series 204). East Melbourne, Victoria, Australia: Centre for Strategic Education.

fundamentalism. (2017). In *Merriam-Webster.com.* Accessed at www.merriam -webster.com/dictionary/fundamentalism on March 3, 2017.

Glanz, B. (2000). Improve morale to increase productivity. *Innovative Leader, 9*(7), 8.

Goldhaber, D., Lavery, L., & Theobald, R. (2015). Uneven playing field? Assessing the teacher quality gap between advantaged and disadvantaged students. *Educational Researcher, 44*(5), 293–307. Accessed at http://journals.sagepub .com/doi/pdf/10.3102/0013189X15592622 on February 28, 2017.

Green, R. L. (2005). *ExpectA+tions: How teacher expectations can increase student achievement and assist in closing the achievement gap.* Columbus, OH: McGraw-Hill SRA.

Greene, P. (2017, January 3). *The Every Student Succeeds Act solves nothing* [Blog post]. Accessed at www.huffingtonpost.com/peter-greene/the-every-student-succeed_b_8905710.html on May 8, 2017.

Grissom, J. A., Nicholson-Crotty, S., & Harrington, J. R. (2014). *Estimating the effects of No Child Left Behind on teachers' work environments and job attitudes.* Nashville, TN: Vanderbilt University.

Gruenert, S., & Whitaker, T. (2015). *School culture rewired: How to define, assess, and transform it.* Alexandria, VA: Association for Supervision and Curriculum Development.

Guisbond, L. (2012). *NCLB's lost decade for educational progress: What can we learn from this policy failure?* Jamaica Plain, MA: FairTest.

Haberman, M. (2005). Teacher burnout in black and white. *The New Educator, 1*(3), 153–175.

Hattie, J. (2012). *Visible learning for teachers: Maximizing impact on learning.* New York: Routledge.

Helfand, D. (2005, November 17). Report says teacher union contracts are holding schools back. *Los Angeles Times.* Accessed at http://articles.latimes.com/2005/nov/17/local/me-teach17 on June 29, 2017.

Herrnstein, R. J., & Murray, C. (1994). *The bell curve: Intelligence and class structure in American life.* New York: Free Press.

Higgins, L., & Pratt-Dawsey, C. (2008, April 23). Changes to No Child unveiled. *Detroit Free Press, 117,* 1.

Hill, D. M., & Barth, M. (2004). NCLB and teacher retention: Who will turn out the lights? *Education and the Law, 16*(2–3), 173–181.

Hudson, C. G. (2005). Socioeconomic status and mental illness. *American Journal of Orthopsychiatry, 75*(1), 14–17.

Hughes, A. L., Matt, J. J., & O'Reilly, F. L. (2015). Principal support is imperative to the retention of teachers in hard-to-staff schools. *Journal of Education and Training Studies, 3*(1), 129–134. Accessed at http://files.eric.ed.gov/fulltext/EJ1054905.pdf on March 2, 2017.

Hunt, J. (2003). *Teacher retention biggest school woe.* Accessed at www.cnn.com/2003/EDUCATION/01/29/teacher.shortage.ap on July 19, 2008.

Infoplease. (2006). *African-Americans by the numbers: U.S. Census.* Accessed at www.infoplease.com/spot/bhmcensus1.html on September 9, 2008.

Ingersoll, R., Merrill, L., & Stuckey, D. (2014). *Seven trends: The transformation of the teaching force, updated April 2014* (CPRE Report #RR-80). Philadelphia: Consortium for Policy Research in Education, University of Pennsylvania. Accessed at www.cpre.org/sites/default/files/workingpapers /1506_7trendsapril2014.pdf on February 28, 2017.

Jackson, Y. (2011). *The pedagogy of confidence: Inspiring high intellectual performance in urban schools.* New York: Teachers College Press.

Jencks, C., & Phillips, M. (Eds.). (1998). *The black-white test score gap.* Washington, DC: Brookings Institution Press.

Jochim, A., & McGuinn, P. (2016). The politics of Common Core assessments. *Education Next, 16*(4), 44–52.

Jones, M. T. (2008). *Race/ethnicity and teacher expectations of college attendance.* Presented at the American Sociological Association Annual Conference, Montréal, Québec, Canada.

Jones, S. M., Bouffard, S. M., & Weissbourd, R. (2013). Educators' social and emotional skills vital to learning. *Phi Delta Kappan, 94*(8), 62–65.

Kearney, M. S., & Harris, B. H. (2014). *Report: Ten economic facts about crime and incarceration in the United States.* Washington, DC: Brookings Institution.

Keller, B. (2008). Studies link teacher absences to lower student scores. *Education Week, 27*, 1.

Kennedy, M. (2005). *Inside teaching: How classroom life undermines reform.* Cambridge, MA: Harvard University Press.

Klein, A. (2016, March 31). The Every Student Succeeds Act: An ESSA overview [Opinion]. *Education Week.* Accessed at www.edweek.org/ew/issues /every-student-succeeds-act/index.html on May 8, 2017.

Kopkowski, C. (2008, February). Why they leave: Lack of respect, NCLB, and underfunding—in a topsy-turvy profession, what can make today's teachers stay? *NEA Today.* Accessed at www.nea.org/neatoday/0804/whytheyleave .html on October 27, 2008.

Kunjufu, J. (2002). *Black students, middle class teachers.* Chicago: African American Images.

Ladd, H. F. (n.d.). *Teacher effects: What do we know?* Accessed at www.sesp .northwestern.edu/docs/teacher-quality-1.pdf on February 28, 2017.

Learning Point Associates. (n.d.). *Teacher perceptions, expectations, and behaviors may put black students at a disadvantage.* Accessed at http://lpadev.learningpt .org/gaplibrary/text/teacherperceptions2.php on October 27, 2008.

Lee, T. (2014, May 7). *Education racial gap as wide as ever according to NAEP.* Accessed at www.msnbc.com/msnbc/student-proficiency-stagnant-race -gap-wide on May 8, 2017.

Lencioni, P. (2012). *The advantage: Why organizational health trumps everything else in business.* San Francisco: Jossey-Bass.

Levin, H. (2006). Equity by the numbers. *Phi Delta Kappan, 13,* 53–65.

Lewis, L. (2006). Baltimore program helps new teachers get off to a good start. *Education World, 3,* 11–12.

Lezotte, L. (1999). *Correlates of Effective Schools: The first and second generation.* Okemos, MI: Effective Schools Products. Accessed at www.gulllakecs.org /cms/lib/MI01001276/Centricity/Domain/65/Correlates_of_Effective _Schools.pdf on May 8, 2017.

Lortie, D. C. (1975). *Schoolteacher: A sociological study.* Chicago: University of Chicago Press.

Lortie, D. (2002). *Schoolteacher: A sociological study* (2nd ed.). Chicago: University of Chicago Press.

Loveless, T. (2013). The resurgence of ability grouping and persistence of tracking. In *The 2013 Brown Center report on American education: How well are American children learning?* (pp. 12–20). Washington, DC: Brown Center on Education Policy. Accessed at www.brookings.edu/wp-content /uploads/2016/06/2013-brown-center-report-web-3.pdf on May 8, 2017.

Maccoby, M. (2008). Schools need collaborative leaders. *Education Week, 27*(24), 11.

Maclean, N. (1992). *Young men and fire.* Chicago: University of Chicago Press.

Majumdar, S. (2013, July 19). *India faces growing problem of more skilled workers than jobs.* Accessed at www.rediff.com/business/slide-show/slide -show-1-column-india-faces-growing-problem-of-more-skilled-workers -than-jobs/20130719.htm on May 8, 2017.

Martin, C., & Sargrad, S. (2015, December 3). Leaving behind No Child Left Behind. *U.S. News & World Report.* Accessed at www.usnews .com/opinion/knowledge-bank/2015/12/03/every-student-succeeds-act -is-better-than-no-child-left-behind on February 27, 2017.

Marzano, R. J. (2003). *What works in schools: Translating research into action.* Alexandria, VA: Association for Supervision and Curriculum Development.

Marzano, R. J. (2017). *The new art and science of teaching.* Bloomington, IN: Solution Tree Press.

Marzano, R. J., & Waters, T. (2009). *District leadership that works: Striking the right balance*. Bloomington, IN: Solution Tree Press.

McCarthy-Wood, T., & Wood, C. (2002). *Understanding and preventing teacher burnout. Washington, DC: ERIC Clearinghouse on Teaching and Teacher Education*. (ERIC Document Reproduction Service No. ED477726) Accessed at www.ericdigests.org/2004–1/burnout.htm on October 27, 2008.

Mirel, J., & Goldin, S. (2012, April 17). Alone in the classroom: Why teachers are too isolated. *The Atlantic*. Accessed at www.theatlantic.com/national /archive/2012/04/alone-in-the-classroom-why-teachers-are-too-isolated /255976 on February 28, 2017.

Moire, E. (2008, Winter). Building an effective new teacher support system. *NEA Today: Issues in Education Report, 7*.

Muhammad, A. (2009). *Transforming school culture: How to overcome staff division*. Bloomington, IN: Solution Tree Press.

National Center for Education Statistics. (2015). *The nation's report card: 2015 mathematics and reading assessments*. Accessed at www.nationsreportcard .gov/reading_math_2015/#?grade=4 on May 8, 2017.

National Commission on Teaching and America's Future. (2003). *No dream denied: A pledge to America's children*. Washington, DC: Author.

Nelson, N. C. (2007). *The power of appreciation in business: How an obsession with value increases performance, productivity and profits*. New York: MindLab.

No Child Left Behind Act of 2001, Pub. L. No. 107–110, § 115, Stat. 1425 (2002).

Obama, B. (2008). *The audacity of hope: Thoughts on reclaiming the American dream*. New York: Vintage Books.

Ogbu, J. U. (2003). *Black American students in an affluent suburb: A study of academic disengagement*. New York: Erlbaum Associates.

Ordway, D.-M., & Wihbey, J. (2017). *Negative political ads and their effect on voters: Updated collection of research*. Accessed at https://journalistsresource .org/studies/politics/ads-public-opinion/negative-political-ads-effects -voters-research-roundup on March 3, 2017.

Patterson, K., Grenny, J., McMillan, R., & Switzler, A. (2002). *Crucial conversations: Tools for talking when stakes are high*. New York: McGraw-Hill.

Patterson, K., Grenny, J., McMillan, R., & Switzler, A. (2012). *Crucial conversations: Tools for talking when stakes are high* (2nd ed.). New York: McGraw-Hill.

Pew Research Center. (2016). *On views of race and inequality, blacks and whites are worlds apart.* Washington, DC: Author. Accessed at www.pewsocialtrends .org/2016/06/27/1-demographic-trends-and-economic-well-being on February 27, 2017.

Phillips, O. (2015). *Revolving door of teachers costs schools billions every year.* Accessed at www.npr.org/sections/ed/2015/03/30/395322012/the-hidden -costs-of-teacher-turnover on February 28, 2017.

Proctor, B. D., Semega, J. L., & Kollar, M. A. (2016). *Income and poverty in the United States: 2015—Current population reports.* Washington, DC: U.S. Census Bureau. Accessed at www.census.gov/content/dam/Census /library/publications/2016/demo/p60-256.pdf on May 8, 2017.

Pyöriä, P. (2007). Informal organizational culture: The foundation of knowledge workers' performance. *Journal of Knowledge Management, 11*(3), 16–30.

Rubie-Davies, C. M. (2006). Teacher expectations and student self-perceptions: Exploring relationships. *Psychology in the Schools, 43*(5), 537–552.

Sadovi, C. (2008, September 8). Chicago students skip for a cause. *Chicago Tribune.*

Sahlberg, P. (2011). *Finnish lessons: What can the world learn from educational change in Finland?* New York: Teachers College Press.

Samples, J. (2006). *The fallacy of campaign finance reform.* Chicago: University of Chicago Press.

Sanders, W., & Rivers, J. (1996). *Cumulative and residual effects of teachers on future student academic achievement.* Knoxville: University of Tennessee.

Schmoker, M. (2011). *Focus: Elevating the essentials to radically improve student learning.* Alexandria, VA: Association for Supervision and Curriculum Development.

Shaw, B. (2008, March 12). Our nation still at risk. *Education Week,* 17–18.

Smith, M., Jaffe-Gill, E., Segal, J., & Segal, R. (2007, October 26). *Preventing burnout: Signs, symptoms, and strategies to avoid it.* Accessed at www.helpguide .org/mental/burnout_signs_symptoms.htm on October 27, 2008.

Sparks, D. (2002). *High-performing cultures increase teacher retention.* Oxford, OH: Learning Forward.

Sutcher, L., Darling-Hammond, L., & Carver-Thomas, D. (2016). *A coming crisis in teaching? Teacher supply, demand, and shortages in the U.S.* Palo Alto, CA: Learning Policy Institute.

Tangredi, D. (2005, January 29). Einstein: Definition of insanity. *Ezine Articles*. Accessed at http://ezinearticles.com/?expert=Danny_Tangredi on October 27, 2008.

Toppo, G. (2008, May 1). Study: Reading First has little impact on kids' scores. *USA Today*.

Turner, J. C., Christensen, A., & Meyer, D. K. (2009). Teachers' beliefs about student learning and motivation. In L. J. Saha & A. G. Dworkin (Eds.), *International handbook of research on teachers and teaching* (pp. 361–371). Berlin, Germany: Springer.

Tyack, D., & Cuban, L. (1995). *Tinkering toward utopia: A century of public school reform*. Cambridge, MA: Harvard University Press.

U.S. Department of Defense. (1973). *Military leadership*. Annapolis, MD: Author.

U.S. Department of Education, Office for Civil Rights. (2014a). *Civil Rights Data Collection for the 2013–14 school year*. Washington, DC: Author.

U.S. Department of Education, Office for Civil Rights. (2014b). *Civil Rights Data Collection: Data snapshot—school discipline*. Washington, DC: Author.

Weick, K. E. (1996). Drop your tools: An allegory for organizational studies. *Administrative Science Quarterly, 41*(2), 301–313.

Weick, K. E. (2009). *Making sense of the organization, volume 2: The impermanent organization*. Chichester, England: Wiley.

Wilson, B. L., & Corbett, H. D. (2001). *Listening to urban kids: School reform and the teachers they want*. Albany: State University of New York Press.

Winerip, M. (2007, December 9). In gaps at school, weighing family life. *The New York Times*.

Wynn, S. (2006, April 12). Principal leadership, school climate critical to retaining beginning teachers, Duke study finds. *Duke News*.

Yoeli, E., Hoffman, M., Rand, D. G., & Nowak, M. A. (2013). *Powering up with indirect reciprocity in a large-scale field experiment*. Irvine: University of California, Irvine.

Zuckerbrod, N. (2007, November 15). *City schools gain, but still lag nation*. Accessed at www.thefreelibrary.com/NANCY+ZUCKERBROD-a1449 on October 27, 2008.

Index

171

Transforming School Culture
Anthony Muhammad
Muhammad describes the prevailing beliefs and assumptions of four different types of educators: Believers, Fundamentalists, Tweeners, and Survivors. After arguing that their collective dynamic ultimately determines the culture of a school, he provides specific strategies for working with each group.
DVF022

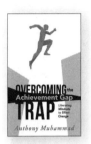

Overcoming the Achievement Gap Trap
Anthony Muhammad
Ensure learning equality in every classroom. Investigate previous and current policies designed to help close the achievement gap. Explore strategies for adopting a new mindset that frees educators and students from negative academic performance expectations.
BKF618

The Will to Lead, the Skill to Teach
Anthony Muhammad, Sharroky Hollie
The authors acknowledge both the structural and sociological issues that contribute to low-performing schools and offer multiple tools and strategies to assess and improve classroom management, increase literacy, establish academic vocabulary, and contribute to a healthier school culture.
BKF443

Timebomb
Mike Mattos
Timebomb is a powerful wake-up call to the urgency of reducing dropout rates and preparing students for a better future. The video's bold message will inspire educators to provide the best education possible by collaborating at high levels and establishing quality support systems.
DVF074

GL●BAL **PD**

Access **Hundreds of Videos & Books** from Top Experts

Global PD gives educators focused and goals-oriented training from top experts. You can rely on this innovative online tool to improve instruction in every classroom.

- Gain job-embedded PD from the largest library of PLC videos and books in the world.

- Customize learning based on skill level and time commitments; videos are less than 20 minutes, and books can be browsed by chapter to accommodate busy schedules.

- Get unlimited, on-demand access—24 hours a day.

▶ **LEARN MORE**
SolutionTree.com/GlobalPDLibrary

Solution Tree